Living the Deepest Truth You Know

Living the Deepest Truth You Know

Albert Bellg

Appleton, Wisconsin

Copyright © 2023 Albert Bellg

All rights reserved. If you copy or quote parts of this book, please cite the source. Thank you for respecting the work that has gone into this book.

Sloan Press
8 Brokaw Place
Appleton, Wisconsin 54911
Sloan Press is an imprint of LifePath LLC

ISBN 978-0-9965103-7-0

eISBN 978-0-9965103-8-7

Library of Congress Control Number: 2023904585

Cover design by Robin Locke Monda
Author photo by Kara Bellg

Set in Arno Pro by Raphaël Freeman MISTD, Renana Typesetting

For my love, Laurin,
and our daughters Katie and Kara –
and with deep gratitude
to the many friends, teachers and guides
who have supported me
in living the deepest truth I know.

Contents

Introduction ix

1. Who Am I, Anyway? 1
2. Trust 17
3. Courage 35
4. Asking for Your Truth 49
5. Understanding Inner Wisdom 67
6. Mission and Purpose 85
7. Welcome, Truth 107
8. Opening to Life 123
9. Fully Alive 137

Appendix: Your Own Journey 151
Gratitude 157
Notes, Comments and References 159

Introduction

One day you finally knew
what you had to do, and began...

– Mary Oliver, "The Journey"

One evening a few years ago, my wife Laurin and I were sitting on our living room couch and talking about an issue that concerned her. She's a physician and I'm a psychologist, and she was trying to decide how to navigate a particularly tricky professional situation with one of her medical colleagues. There were personal issues involved, no easy solutions, no simple way forward. Thinking about different options and ways of approaching the problem in the back and forth of our conversation, I surprised both of us by saying something that suddenly made her sit up and stare at me.

"Write that down," she said urgently. "I want to remember that." This was the only time in our life together that she's said something like that to me, so of course I wrote it down. We even gave it a place of honor on our refrigerator for several months. What I'd said was this:

Find the deepest truth you know
and let everything else fall in place around it.

There is something about those words that just felt right to both of us. For Laurin at that particular moment, they showed her a way through the confusion and allowed her to think clearly about how to handle the issue with her colleague. In the years since then, however, she's used that statement to transform her life. She's become more engaged with people, more confident about taking a leadership role at her work, more at ease speaking up and working with groups, and more willing to take risks and pursue what she truly cares about. It's led her to write a wonderful and successful book about her experiences with her patients – which is something she never thought she would do – and inspired her to go back to school and get a Master of Fine Arts degree in creative writing.

For me, I realized that "find the deepest truth you know and let everything else fall in place around it" is a simple statement of a personal process I've engaged in throughout my life. As I've made important decisions about relationships, where to live, how to pursue my career, what spiritual practice to follow, and whether or not to get involved in other activities, I've nearly always looked inside myself for direction. I may still do a conventional evaluation and weigh the costs and benefits of a particular choice, determine the consensus of expert opinion, follow cultural norms, or sometimes just go along with what other people want me to do. But when I choose to look inward and follow what I call my *inner wisdom*, I am led into some extraordinary and meaningful experiences.

Another gift came for me, too, in the statement I made. I came to understand that it's personally important for me to share with others the process of finding the deepest truth you know. To do that, I also realized that I'd have to make significant changes in my work and my professional identity. At that time, I'd been a clinical health psychologist for nearly two decades, helping people cope with medical issues, make positive lifestyle changes to improve

INTRODUCTION

their health, and resolve their symptoms of depression, anxiety or stress. It was meaningful and worthwhile to me, and to the people I worked with. But as rewarding and satisfying as it had been to help patients with their problems, I had not been guiding them to find the deepest truth in their lives and act on that truth with courage.

So a little over six months after I made that statement to Laurin, I followed my inner wisdom and left a secure job with a corner office in a medical center and moved into a one-person office on a quiet, tree-lined street. It was the perfect place to explore my own inner wisdom and discover how I could work with people to find and live the deepest truth they know. Taking off the professional hat I'd worn for so many years as a health psychologist let me look at this process from a broader perspective, one that embraces what I know of spirituality, writing and literature, nature, my personal experience, and sometimes psychology, as well.

It starts with a simple idea: at the heart of creativity, healing, and personal and spiritual growth is a wise inner knowing. When I've looked for it, inner wisdom has often shown up as a surprising but insightful awareness about a situation I'm in, or a question or issue I'm concerned about. When I've been thoughtful, discerning, and brave enough to follow the insight it offers, the result has been life-changing. Inner wisdom has offered a genuine and whole-hearted way of moving forward in my life.

One way I've found that inner wisdom is distinguished from other ways of knowing is that it often reveals something distinctly beyond what I already know and want, and it reflects a deeper truth about who I am and what I really need. Inner wisdom has helped me – and I believe it can help anyone – decide what career to pursue, find a good place to live, be a better parent and partner, engage more deeply in spiritual or religious practice, solve problems, be creative, write in a more personal and authentic way, and heal emotional wounds. There is also abundant evidence beyond my own experience that inner wisdom can give genuine insight into what is going on around us and in us, and help us discover what to do next.

My inner wisdom has done more than guide my decisions and actions, however. It has also been part of my spiritual path, and it has profoundly changed my sense of myself and my relationships with others. In much the same way that I have been blessed to experience the personal change that happens by loving someone and creating a committed relationship, I have also seen the deep transformation that's possible when making a committed relationship to inner wisdom and true self. As you read this book, I hope that you will be intrigued by the same questions that inspired me: What will change inside me when I start to love and trust my inner wisdom? How will I be different when, every day, I look to my inner wisdom for guidance? What happens when I begin to identify with that part of myself, and let my true self be who I am in the world?

There is something both wonderful and humbling about bringing inner wisdom into your daily life, relationships, work, spirituality, and community – what I call *living the deepest truth you know*. In these pages, I offer my thoughts about how you can become more aware of your inner wisdom in a conscious, intentional and discerning way, and what you can do to make the deepest truth you know the foundation for how you live.

Like my life, this book has its own shape and character, influenced by the joys that have illuminated me and the deep hurts I have grown from and healed. My own spiritual journey and personal experiences, along with a few of my poems, are woven throughout it in a way that I hope will be helpful. I've also included stories from people I've worked with as a psychologist (with their names and circumstances altered), the insights and learnings that have come from facilitating retreats, and the stories and thoughts

INTRODUCTION

of my friends and fellow explorers who are making the deepest truth they know central to their lives.

Living the deepest truth you know in daily life is challenging, and I've not always been successful at it. You, too, may find it difficult to stay on the living edge of your inner wisdom. To do that as best you can, you need to develop trust in your inner wisdom and be willing to courageously follow a path that others may not understand. You may also need to let go of conventional ways of thinking, heal old hurts, and forgive yourself and others. The gift when you do – along with a sense of aliveness, connection with others, and peace – is a life that's truly your own.

Albert Bellg
Appleton, Wisconsin
May, 2023

*There is something in every one of you that waits,
listens for the sound of the genuine in yourself –
and if you cannot hear it, you will never find
whatever it is for which you are searching.*

– Howard Thurman
1980 Commencement Address
Spelman College

Chapter 1

Who Am I, Anyway?

To be nobody-but-yourself – in a world which is doing its best, night and day, to make you everybody else – means to fight the hardest battle which any human being can fight; and never stop fighting.

– E.E. Cummings, *A Poet's Advice to Students*

When I graduated from college, I had no idea what I'd do to make a living. With my shiny new bachelor's degree in English and a handful of poems I'd written, I had vague but ambitious thoughts of working for a magazine or small newspaper as a proofreader or even a junior editor. I moved to Milwaukee where my friend Steve lived, found a cheap apartment to share with four other people, and started sending out letters and making phone calls. But nobody seemed interested in hiring me, or even talking to me. After a few weeks, I began to worry about how I would pay my share of the rent.

Feeling ashamed that I'd failed horribly at even the first step of making my way in the world as I thought I should, I got a job as a house painter. I'd painted my family's garage when I was in high school and thought that maybe I could support myself painting houses. But I was afraid of heights. When my boss, a kind but practical Polish immigrant who'd been a professional painter for twenty years, discovered I could only work on short ladders or with my feet on the ground, he let me go. However, in the seven or eight days that I worked for him, he taught me the proper way to use a paint brush and cut in windows – and fortunately, my landlady had some interiors she wanted me to paint in the houses she owned around town. I couldn't afford a car, so, dressed in painter's whites and juggling cans of paint, rollers and brushes, I rode a bicycle or took the bus to wherever I was working that day.

As confused and disappointed as I was about my career, though, something else was going on. Those poems I'd written in college still meant something to me. In fact, the satisfaction I got from putting my thoughts and feelings down on paper felt more meaningful and real to me than anything else I did. Writing was how I discovered what was going on inside myself, and at that time in my life, I had no other way to do that. So almost every day, usually in the morning shortly after I woke up, I sat down and worked on a poem or wrote a page or two of prose, slowly revealing to myself how I saw things and who I was.

Once I started the hard physical work of painting houses (it doesn't look hard, but it is when you do it all day long under the pressure of a deadline), I discovered that I was too tired to write. Painting is a daytime job, and putting in enough hours required me to start work early in the morning, my best time for writing. I had a choice to make: keep painting houses (which I knew could pay the rent), or continue to write. As important as it was to have a place to live, something in me knew that I had to keep writing and make it the priority over everything else. It was the only thing I was doing then that mattered to me, and I simply had to keep doing it, no matter what. Which meant that I needed to find another job.

With that clarity, things just fell into place. Steve told me about a second shift factory job that had opened up in the chemical company where he worked as a junior research chemist. I applied for the position and became a bulk weigher, carefully measuring chemicals out of large containers into small ones for resale. The job started at 3:30 in the afternoon, which gave me time to write in the morning, and paid better than the minimum wage. But I had mixed feelings about accepting it. The person who'd had the job before me had died in an explosion while repackaging a chemical. I tried to reassure myself that there were now better safety procedures in place – and such a thing couldn't happen twice, could it? Still, even if I didn't blow up, I was being exposed to nasty carcinogenic chemicals and other hazards. I vowed to keep the job for no more than six months.

But the bulk weigher job let me write, and that's what mattered. It gave me my mornings when I felt the most creative, and it wasn't so physically or emotionally demanding that it made me too tired to think. In that first year after I graduated, I finished a draft of a very bad novel (mercifully never published) and enough poems to print a small collection. I ran off fifty copies of my poetry chapbook at a cheap commercial print shop and sold them for a dollar.

More importantly, I began to see that how much money I made and how successful I was by conventional standards didn't have to be what my life was about. Choosing to explore my inner world and write about things that mattered to me, and even to think of myself as a writer, wasn't about getting published, making money or becoming famous. It was more personal and important than that. Writing was a way to discover who I was and live in a way that was true to myself. That personal exploration took priority over any expectations about how I should live. In the language I use now, it was the first time I made the choice to live the deepest truth I know and let everything else fall in place around it.

The hardest battle

Choosing to make time to write was challenging and life-changing for me, but fortunately, it didn't create significant conflict with other people in my life. This isn't always the case after you discover the truth about who you are or what you need to do. It can be dangerous to talk about – and even riskier to act on – the deepest truth you know. Sharing who you really are and what you truly think and feel, if you can do it at all, is usually confined to those you feel safe with, if you're fortunate enough to have such people in your life. Even when you do, though, sometimes close friends, family members or others who usually support you will not like it when you express and act on your inner truth. You may be in direct conflict with their beliefs or with what they need you to be or do for them.

When circumstances or relationships keep you from expressing or acting on what is true for you, you no longer live in integrity. You suffer the pain and stress of a divided life: a life that's different on the outside than it is on the inside. At its extreme, this division between who you are inside and who you feel required to be on the outside can become a painful betrayal of what you genuinely care about and of who you truly are. That inner torment is often called *living a lie*. Sadly, sometimes tragically, nearly all of us live a lie at some point in our lives.

There are many reasons you might feel forced to live a divided life, or at worst, a lie. It's not at all uncommon for relationships with family members, bosses and co-workers, people at church, or friends to be at risk if you speak or act on what feels true and real to you. The price of expressing your truth may be anger, rejection, divorce, or being disowned. It can lead to the loss of income, inheritance, or love. And what if the people you love tell you that the truth about who you are, what you think, how you do things, who you love, or what you believe is a ticket to eternal damnation and hell?

The pressures to deny your truth and even to avoid being aware of it are often enormous. Yet the quiet inner demand to know your truth, express it and live it is one of the most powerful forces inside you. How you come to grips with that conflict and resolve it – how you "fight the hardest battle which any human being can fight," as poet E.E. Cummings said – is one of the universal human challenges. The way you meet this challenge in large part will define who you are and how you live your life.

Listening deeply

The first few years after I graduated from college weren't a particularly happy time. I often felt inadequate and unsure of myself, and I almost gave up my morning writing time so I could get a better job. In the early days when I still doubted what I was doing and struggled with the thought that I should have a better job and be making more money, I took the U.S. Federal Civil Service examination. I scored well enough to be offered a job as a clerk in the Social Security Administration. The irony of this didn't escape me, and with very mixed feelings, I accepted the job over the phone. But after a sleepless night, I called the next morning and said I'd changed my mind. Taking that job would have helped me feel more "socially secure," but it also felt like living a lie and abandoning the writing that I cared about. I couldn't bring myself to do that. A few weeks later, I was offered an even better paying job as a civilian with the U.S. Navy. I turned that down, too.

Seeing clearly that I needed to refuse those substantial and secure job opportunities – and working up the courage to actually do it – felt like an even greater challenge than arranging my work schedule so I could write. When I did take that step, though, I felt that I'd passed a kind of inner test. It felt good to affirm my commitment to the time I needed for creative work and to organize my life around my writing.

After I'd worked a few months at the chemical company,

my inner wisdom began nudging me with the idea of moving someplace else. Rationally, a city like Chicago, New York, Seattle or San Francisco made the most sense for someone who wanted to be a writer. But my attention was drawn to, of all places, Kansas City, Missouri. Even though I didn't know much about it and had never been there, it felt right in a deeper way than I could explain. So after reading about the city to quiet my doubts and justify following that inner prompting – Kansas City was getting a lot of good press at the time – that's where I went.

When I got off the bus with two suitcases and $300, I knew that I immediately needed to find an inexpensive place to live and a job. I also knew that I needed to find a t'ai chi instructor. The job and a place to live made sense, of course. But what urgently called me to learn t'ai chi was more puzzling. I'd had no experience of it at all, other than seeing it once on television: Chinese people in a park, moving slowly. I'd been a soccer player in high school and college, moving hard and fast, kicking a ball, and mixing it up physically with the other players. Once again, the insistent call of this activity was beyond any rational explanation I had for it, but I knew I needed to do t'ai chi.

I found a city bus to the student union of the University of Missouri-Kansas City. From my past experience on college campuses, I was pretty sure it would have a housing bulletin board listing apartments and rooms for rent at reasonable prices. I found a cheap, not-quite-bug-free one-bedroom apartment in a dilapidated old building with mostly poor, elderly tenants. A couple of days after settling in, I found a part-time position ringing a cash register in a drug store. When I applied for the job, I told my boss that I wasn't available to work until 11 a.m. or later – and he still hired me! So I had work that covered my expenses and gave me my mornings to write. A week or so later, I found a t'ai chi class just a few blocks away. Then I discovered that my apartment was across the street from an organization led by a wild-haired

Gestalt therapist, where a group for writers was starting. Things were working out.

The inner prompting to do t'ai chi was very wise, and I'm glad I took it seriously. I immediately felt a profound connection with the physical and mental experience of t'ai chi and practiced it intently every day. Clearly, something in me was changing for the better. Inner distractions and restlessness had made it difficult for me to meditate when I was in college, but t'ai chi was a physical activity, and I found it easier to relax my body and calm my mind as I focused on its slow, graceful movements. I became aware of how stiff and tense I was, and my body started to become more flexible and free. I was less worried and anxious. I began to see why I had been drawn to t'ai chi when I knew almost nothing about it. I even became a t'ai chi instructor for several years and had some great experiences teaching it to people with physical disabilities.

A few months after I arrived in Kansas City, I was seriously tempted to change the path I was on. Back when I was floundering and had taken the Civil Service exam, I had also applied to several Master of Fine Arts (MFA) programs in creative writing. Being a student had always been the default setting in my life, so why not go back to school and study writing? Sure enough, a few months after I arrived in Kansas City, I received a letter saying that I was accepted into an MFA program at San Francisco State University. But even though it made a kind of sense to pursue another degree, it felt wrong to leave Kansas City. The inner guidance that got me there had quite remarkably connected me with the experiences and people that I needed, including other writers, so it didn't feel right to go back into an academic environment that was maybe a little too familiar and safe. I knew that leaving to pursue an academic path at that time would separate me from the fragile inner process I was engaged in to discover myself as a person and live from my deepest truth. After considerable soul searching, I stayed where I was.

Those early experiences of following my inner promptings taught me some important things. I learned, to my surprise, that the right answers for my life were not "out there," determined by others or by the expectations of society. The best choices for how I needed to live could not be found by reading about what most people like and do, or by doing things that didn't matter to me but that made me look successful or allowed me to make more money. I learned that if I paid attention to what I cared about inside and was brave enough to act on it, I could find a way to live that was true to myself.

A few years after I moved to Kansas City, I was driving a car I'd borrowed from a friend. I still remember exactly where I was, the curve and gentle rise of the road in front of me in Gillham Park near the Nelson Art Gallery, trees and grass on each side. In that moment, a sense of joy came over me, and I felt alive and grateful. I was genuinely happy with my life. There was a richness and depth to what I was doing and who I was becoming, and it felt good to be me.

Those experiences in Milwaukee and Kansas City are where it started. I wouldn't have put it this way back then, but it was becoming clear that if I was willing to be guided by the deepest truth I knew, I would be aligned with a larger, deeper reality and connected with the resources and experiences I needed. As I developed confidence in my inner wisdom when making important decisions and committed myself to following it, this way of doing things made me less fearful in my interactions with others and more willing to try new things. As I opened to my inner truth in the decades that followed, I was happier, more secure, and more genuine, even when my deepest truth led me down some unusual and challenging paths.

What is "the deepest truth you know"?

I realize that I'm claiming a lot when I use the phrase "the deepest truth you know" to describe what I was experiencing. How did I know that my simple desire to be a writer and move from one city to another was something as grand as my "deepest truth" – and what does the word "truth" mean here, anyway? In fact, what I mean by "the deepest truth you know" in this book is quite specific and worth describing in detail.

The deepest truth you know is the deep knowing or experiencing of something being true that comes to you, perhaps surprisingly, in the present moment. Depending on your background, you may believe that this experience of truth comes from God or a spiritual part of yourself, or that it's an unconscious cognitive process resulting from other experiences you've had, the knowledge you've accumulated, the demands or values of others that you've internalized, or something else. I'll discuss some of those possibilities later. But the first thing to say about the deepest truth you know is that it's a deep inner knowing in the present moment that something is right or true.

Not everything you know to be true is the deepest truth you know. For instance, the experience of truth I'm talking about is not a pre-existing fact, belief or feeling that you can take down from the shelf, dust off, and hold up for everyone to see, even if it happens to be immensely important or useful to you. For example, the deepest truth I know is not a fact such as "I love my wife and children" or "the best way to get to the airport from where I live is to go west on College Avenue." It is not a belief, even one that I consider fundamental and meaningful to my life, such as "God is love" or "the scientific method is one of the best ways to attain reliable information about the world."

It's also not just having positive or strong feelings about something. "Doing what you love" may be a pretty good guideline for choosing a career and loving someone is essential to a close relationship or a marriage, but those feelings about a particular job or person are not the deepest truth you know. Similarly, it's not the ideas and beliefs you're most passionate about, or the heady and often arrogant sense that you're absolutely right about something. It's not the deep understanding you might have about something because you know it well. It's not the well-informed opinion of an expert, the wise words from a guru or teacher, or even the scientific consensus about a topic. Nor does the deepest truth you know come from a political leader or religious authority, or from a religious text such as the Bible or the Koran.

As I want to explore it here, the deepest truth you know is an often-unexpected experience of insight, realization, or understanding – an *ahh…* moment of recognition, an *ah-ha!* moment of revelation, or perhaps even a *what?* moment of surprise – that you have in the present, right now. That insight or realization is usually about something that's personally important, such as a relationship, a life decision, or a difficult situation you're facing that's led you to feel unsettled, emotionally distressed, or even physically uneasy about your issue. A "deepest truth" insight often has a specific effect: it frequently resolves your confusion or distress and leads to a sense of deeper understanding, peace or resolution.

After experiencing what feels like the deepest truth you know, you face two challenges: discerning whether it's the real thing, and deciding how to act on it. Discernment is necessary because humans have a remarkable capacity for self-deception, and you need to determine whether an insight you've received is not just what you already want, know or feel. This requires making a commitment to practice personal reflection and develop self-understanding. You may need to reduce your attachment to what you think you know and want, discover the ways your thoughts and beliefs are blind to significant aspects of reality, and develop a degree of spiritual maturity. These are no small tasks – but in my experience, once you learn to recognize it, inner wisdom can be an intimate part of your personal growth that meets you exactly where you are in your life.

The second challenge is to decide how to take action on your insight. To act on your wise inner knowing, or "to live the deepest truth you know," may go against the social expectations and demands of the people you live with or the personal expectations you have for yourself, and therefore take considerable trust and courage. I certainly struggled with following my inner wisdom when I was starting out, and still sometimes do. But when you have the clarity to be aware of it and courage to act on it, you live in integrity with what is real and true for you.

Your inner wisdom can surprise you. In a moment of personal crisis or change, it can spontaneously come forward to give you new insight to help you survive or make the right decision. But you can also deliberately cultivate inner wisdom through your own contemplative practice or inner work, or through a personal encounter with something that inspires you, such as art, poetry or nature. That deliberate process might also be an interaction with someone you're close to such as an insightful friend, mentor, spiritual director, or psychological counselor, or even a group process designed to help people connect with their insight and inner wisdom.

One fascinating aspect of the personal experience of inner wisdom is that it can present itself in many ways. It may come in words that you hear or are aware of inside yourself, as internal visual images or symbols, a heightened awareness of something in your environment, an inner sense of rightness or affirmation, a physical sensation such as a tingling or vibration, a sudden and unexpected emotion, or as a memory that is relevant to understanding the present. You can also gain insight simply by reflecting on your life experiences. As Quakers say, you might see "way closing" or "way opening" – that is, how your path through life has evolved as you've moved away from some things and toward others, and what you're ready for next, based on that understanding. I have personally experienced my inner wisdom in all of these ways, and I'm sure there are other ways it may show up as well.

When and how your deepest truth shows up is often part of what you need to learn in life and how you are growing as a person. Even *not* immediately getting an insight may be part of an inwardly-guided process of letting your life unfold in the way it needs to. For instance, you may need to learn how to deal more patiently with anxiety or uncertainty without being reassured by your inner wisdom. Or if you've repeatedly avoided taking action on things that are important, you may need to learn more about acting with courage before you receive an insight about something important that you need to do. Many of the insights I've received have come to me in the moment I needed them, but others have come after a longer process of exploration, personal growth, and learning.

The meaning of an insight may not always be clear. As with a dream, you may need to live with an insight for a while, talk about it with others, or simply let life play itself out before you understand what it means. It may not offer an easy or direct answer to your question or issue, which can be frustrating. However, the deepest truth you know doesn't present itself in an incomprehensible foreign language or as a complex mathematical equation. As you live your life, you develop your own particular ways of understanding yourself and communicating with the world around you, and the deepest truth you know will show up in a form and context you're able to comprehend. Your inner wisdom may surprise or challenge you, but it will offer insight that you're ready to know in a way that you're able to know it.

Experiencing your deepest truth

As I started looking for them, I found many examples of other people following their deepest truth, sometimes in the most difficult situations. I was particularly delighted to find a description of following the deepest truth you know in Elizabeth Gilbert's wonderful autobiography, *Eat Pray Love*. Early in her book, she recalled a time when she was in a great deal of emotional pain and considering divorcing her husband. Sobbing on her bathroom floor in the middle of the night, she tried to pray and repeatedly begged God to tell her what she should do. Then she suddenly felt a stillness enfold her, and she stopped crying. In her mind, she heard her own voice calmly, compassionately and lovingly tell her: *Go back to bed, Liz*. She instantly, and with great relief, realized the wisdom of this advice. She knew she wasn't able to make a major decision about her life at that moment, and it made complete sense to her that she needed to rest so she was ready for whatever came next. As she put it, "True wisdom gives the only possible answer at any given moment." That experience opened for her an ongoing connection and conversation with what she understands as the divine.

I found that inner wisdom can help you survive when your life is at risk. I have the pleasure of knowing Joe McMoneagle, a remarkably intuitive and insightful man who was formerly in military intelligence. In his autobiography, *The Stargate Chronicles*, he recalled many times in combat during the Vietnam war when paying attention to what he calls his "inner voices" enabled him to survive an attack. Listening to his inner prompting when he was threatened by enemy fire, he would move his position or jump into a bunker. Often, it was clear within seconds exactly why he was guided to do what he did. Describing a vicious firefight north of Qui Nhon, he noted that his inner voices repeatedly led him to shift his position from locations that moments later were obliterated by mortar rounds or rocket-propelled grenades. He developed a practice of simply following his inner voices even when he might look foolish or embarrassed to do what they said. His strategy was so obviously successful at keeping him out of harm's way, however, that other soldiers noticed and began to do what he did.

Inner wisdom can also help you make career decisions, even when it seems like an awkward choice to others. Vontae Davis, a Pro Bowl cornerback who'd played for ten years in the National Football League, was starting his first game after being traded to the Buffalo Bills. He'd prepared for the game mentally as he usually did, saying to himself that he was going to have the best game of his life. But during the first half of the game, he had what he described as a "spiritual moment" and heard a voice tell him: *I have given all I've got. Leave this chapter behind.* At halftime in the locker room, he put on his street clothes, texted his wife that he was done playing football, and went home. Some of his teammates accused him of being disrespectful and abandoning them in the middle of the game, and sports commentators had a lot to say about it as well. He also gave up several million dollars he would have received for playing the rest of the season. What was more important to him, however, was the deepest truth he knew about his career: it was time to let it go.

These three remarkable examples show just a few of the possibilities for how our inner wisdom might show up. However, they only describe experiences that people had of it individually, by themselves. Just before I completed the first draft of this book, I discovered Parker Palmer's extraordinary book, *A Hidden Wholeness: The Journey Toward an Undivided Life.* What it showed me was that the experience of inner wisdom isn't confined to the moments of individual contemplation and discernment that I had experienced but can also be facilitated in a way I hadn't thought possible: in a group with other people.

After reading Parker's book (I now know him well enough to

call him that), I realized that I needed to stop writing *this* book until I learned more about that intriguing group process. In fact, if I were really going to "get it," my inner wisdom was clear that I needed to become a retreat facilitator with his organization, the Center for Courage & Renewal. But even after I went through a transformational two-year preparation process, it took several more years of facilitating groups and retreats before I felt that I understood enough about what I was doing (and the ways of being that I needed to adopt as a person) to include what I'd learned in these pages. During those years, other things called to me as well, and I learned more about contemplative practices and the unique spirituality of Quakers. They, too, became part of my life and this book.

Even so, this isn't about some special experience available only to those who have the right training or spiritual affiliation, or who've read the right books (including this one!). Letting yourself be guided by your inner wisdom is something that anyone can do. People with all sorts of backgrounds and life experiences find that they can cultivate insight around important questions and issues. There is abundant evidence that when you seek your deepest truth with honest intention and genuine need, it can guide your daily activities, creative process, life decisions, and relationships in remarkable and positive ways.

This is a prose poem I wrote in college. It's one of the pieces that said to me: yes, it's worth making writing a major part of your life. As I read it now, it also foreshadows my understanding of the distinction between the "clear articulation" of the rational mind and inner wisdom's more subtle "faint mental color" – both of which can redefine everything.

THIS IS AN EMPTY SPACE

this is an empty space with perhaps, if you listen carefully, a little music in it, and with all the subtle whorls and patterns the mind sees in empty space when there is no clear articulation of speech or faint mental color that suddenly fills it like an earthquake, jarring and redefining everything – until the painful new horizons fade, and the mind accepts them and says, *ahh, this is easy*... this is an empty space with perhaps, if you listen carefully, a little music in it

Chapter 2

Trust

To have faith is to trust yourself to the water. When you swim, you don't grab the water, because if you do you will sink and drown. Instead you relax, and float.

– Alan Watts

My first apartment in Kansas City had stark white walls and a bare wood floor with almost no furniture except for a bed I built out of a piece of plywood and a mattress, a table, and two chairs I got at a thrift store. It was perfect, I told myself, for a writer who didn't want to be distracted. This was before the day of personal computers, and I had my high school graduation gift from my parents, a manual typewriter, permanently set up and ready to go on the kitchen table. I also had an old-style stainless-steel coffee percolator and kept a pot of strong coffee on the pilot light centered between the four burners of the gas stove. I discovered that if I let it stay hot overnight, the coffee reduced in volume by about a third. By the time I was ready for my first cup in the morning as I sat down to write, it had developed a kick like a Missouri mule. Oddly, it wasn't bitter at all. Through some unknown magic, it also became incredibly smooth and rich-tasting.

It was the perfect elixir to spark a poem that wanted to be written in those early morning hours.

As sparse a life as I was living, things were going well. I'd found an apartment, a job, a t'ai chi class, and fellow writers to work with and learn from. The inner wisdom that led me to Kansas City had clearly been confirmed, and I was trusting it even more. That trust in my inner wisdom also gave me confidence to spread my wings and take the risk of finding out what it was like to be part of a writing community and publish my work. I helped start a weekly writers group, published poems in "little" magazines, created a quarterly newsletter for area writers, brought poetry to elementary and high school students as a Missouri Arts Council "Poet in the Schools," administered a poetry contest in which local poets wrote about artwork at the Nelson Art Gallery, hosted a video series at William Jewell College about author Richard Rhodes, taught creative writing at an organization called the Renaissance Library, and volunteered to read submissions to the local university's literary magazine, *New Letters*. I also wrote and published my first book, which was on soccer tactics for people who wanted to coach a team at the high school level but didn't know much about the game. Getting a book in print was encouraging, and it also gave me a bit more credibility with my writer friends, who were all more accomplished and published than I was.

Back to school

After I had immersed myself in the Kansas City writing community for a few years and gotten more engaged with my own writing, I started to become fascinated with the creative process. How do we come up with new ideas? What are we doing inwardly when we draw, paint, write, or compose music? How do we find creative solutions to problems? It's a process that still intrigues me, and I've come to see that it has many similarities with the process of cultivating inner wisdom. All I wanted to do back then, though, was learn more about it.

I'd read a few articles and books about creativity, but that didn't seem to be enough. To my surprise, I was feeling drawn toward something I thought I'd put behind me: getting a graduate degree. My brain had a way of rationalizing it, too. It came to me that by getting a master's degree, I would be qualified to teach at a university as an adjunct faculty member. Teaching just a few hours a week, I could make as much money as I did selling sporting goods and stringing tennis racquets, my part-time job at the time. I would also be teaching things I liked and cared about.

The only catch was, the place to study the creative process wasn't in an English department. I felt that I was being led to go back to school and get a master's degree in psychology, with a focus on how human beings come up with new ideas and solve problems as individuals and in groups. And unfortunately, I hadn't taken a single psychology course as an undergraduate. After talking it over with the chair of the psychology department at the University of Missouri-Kansas City, he agreed to let me into their program if I first completed all the undergraduate courses necessary for a psychology major. In my state of mind at the time, that seemed like no big deal. I cheerfully committed myself to going back to school for almost three years.

I also needed to pay the rent while I was there. I enrolled in UMKC's work-study program and went over to *New Letters* magazine to see if there was something there for me to do that the work-study program would pay for. It turned out that the magazine's editor, poet David Ray, was leaving in a few weeks to become a visiting professor at another university for a year, and the weekly literary radio program he had just started at the university's public radio station didn't have anyone to keep it going. According to some of my friends, I have an "FM radio" voice. The staff at New Letters put those two things together with my availability, and I ended up working for two-and-a-half years at KCUR-FM as the producer and sometime host for *New Letters On The Air*.

This was one of the most remarkable experiences I had in Kansas City. I interviewed some truly excellent writers on the air, and the show gave them the opportunity to read their work to a radio audience. I was involved with about forty episodes during the time I worked there, learned how to run the board in the studio and mix music with our interviews, and helped the show become one of the first locally-produced programs syndicated nationally via NPR's new satellite. As a young writer, I found it inspiring to be around such fine poets and authors – and as a public radio host and producer with a weekly program, I had one of the most creatively satisfying times of my life.

The most important reason I believe my inner wisdom led me to go back to school, though, was about my future work, but not in the way I'd anticipated. From a rational perspective, had it really made sense to spend several years getting a master's degree just so I could teach part-time and make as little money as I already made? Probably not. In fact, after I got my degree, I never felt motivated to teach regularly at a university as a part-time faculty member. However, by getting a master's degree in psychology, I obtained the credential I would need to follow the inspiration I received eight years later to pursue a Ph.D. in clinical psychology and work with physicians and medical patients. The beautifully guided first step that I took in Kansas City on that hidden path eventually changed my life profoundly, and all while I thought that I was setting myself up to make a living with a part-time, low-level teaching job.

Moving again

After living for six years in Kansas City, I'd finished a master's degree and produced two nationally syndicated radio programs. The second one, *Thresholds of Science*, was offered to me by my KCUR radio friend Mark Morelli, who had originally gotten the idea and funding for it but had to move on before he could produce it himself. That program was on the air for only six months before our funding ran out, but in that short time it won a Corporation for Public Broadcasting award (Honorable Mention) for locally produced educational programs. I regretted that I couldn't find another backer for the program, but the truth is, I didn't look very hard. I was again feeling that it was time to move.

For several years, I'd been involved with a small meditation group led by my friend Jerry Epps, who I'd met when he attended one of the classes I offered in t'ai chi. I liked and respected Jerry in part because he was clearly connected with his own inner wisdom, went to some lengths to follow it, and supported others in doing so with their own spiritual guidance. He taught a meditation practice that focused on connecting with a loving presence deep within, and it helped me become more positive and peaceful.

After a few years of meeting and meditating together, the eight of us in Jerry's meditation group decided to move to Colorado and set up a small cooperative community with a mission of living a more spiritual life and helping others do so as well. We thought about it carefully. It took months of talk and sorting things out (what I would now consider a process of individual and group discernment) to create a shared vision of what we were doing. I was surprised that I didn't feel a call to move to Colorado specifically, but our inner work was connecting deeply with me and I was drawn to our meditation practice and mission. I also felt that I'd finished at least some part of my process of self-discovery that involved being a writer, and this new approach to my inner work was personally meaningful to me. Trusting the process, I made a commitment to take this next step with the group.

Then Jerry suggested a new possibility. Even though it ran counter to all the conversations we'd had about the move, he quite courageously told us that his own inner wisdom was now suggesting that the group split up, with some moving to Tucson and some to Atlanta. He encouraged us to consult our own inner guidance and choose for ourselves where we wanted to go, or if we wanted to go at all. However, as soon as he said "Atlanta," all of the lights came on for me in a way they hadn't for Colorado. In much the same way I'd felt a strong pull to move to Kansas City from Milwaukee, I knew that Atlanta was the next place I needed to be.

As it happened, I was the only person in the group who felt called to move to Atlanta. I'd had enough positive experiences following my inner wisdom to trust it and feel confident that I could make the move, even though, as with Kansas City, I'd never been there. I also felt that by going through the challenging group process that resulted in us making a commitment to move to Colorado, we all had deepened our trust in our inner work and loosened our personal attachments to where we were. Once we had crossed that threshold, it was easier for each of us to discern for ourselves where we wanted to go, Atlanta or Tucson, or if we wanted to stay where we were.

Trusting inner wisdom

Learning to trust your inner wisdom is a key part of the challenge of following it. By its nature, your inner wisdom is not always going to lead you to do things that make sense in an ordinary way. You may have trouble justifying those actions to other people or even to yourself. My own experience early on was that I was a little self-conscious and embarrassed to say when my inner wisdom was prompting me to do something. So I would come up with a fairly conventional (but still true) story that I hoped would make sense to other people. Something like, "I've decided to move to Kansas City to explore something new and focus on my writing." Or, "I'm moving to Atlanta to change gears – I want to see what's next for me." My explanations were honest as far as they went, but they weren't the whole truth. The whole truth would have included the fact that I felt drawn to move to a new city for reasons I couldn't explain but that felt deeply right to me.

The more difficult challenge was trusting the impulse to move and having the courage to act on it. In thinking through the guidance to move to Atlanta, I did an assessment of myself. I was twenty-eight years old. I had good friends in Kansas City, a former girlfriend I was still close to, and owned a house. I was involved in local and regional writing activities and becoming known in the writing community, and hosted a respected and nationally distributed public radio program. I also was part of a group led by a former student of architect Frank Lloyd Wright, where I taught classes and was learning a lot of interesting ideas about how we design our living space and our cities. I could have sought funding to continue working in public radio, looked for a regular teaching position at a local university, or even applied for a writing job at Hallmark Cards, where a number of my friends worked. Perhaps the strongest pull to stay came from my writer's group, which I still enjoyed for its comradery and support.

So I had many reasons to continue my life in Kansas City. But my deepest truth made it possible to hold my external circumstances lightly. What I'd done had been meaningful to me, but the insight leading me forward was more important than building on my accomplishments. Something about Atlanta was calling to me, and I trusted the call enough to follow it.

A place to live

Before I could move to Atlanta, I decided I needed to find a place to live. In retrospect, I'm not sure this was entirely necessary. I could have hitched up a small trailer to my car and driven to Atlanta with my few possessions and my cat and stayed at a cheap hotel while I looked for an apartment I could move into immediately. But something in me wanted to fly in and spend a long weekend in Atlanta, find an apartment, and then return to Kansas City to pack up and make the move, so that's what I did.

I arrived on a Wednesday, with a return ticket for the following Monday morning. As my plane approached the Atlanta airport, I was impressed with how green the city appeared. Aside from the tall buildings downtown, it was almost like a forest, with a few rooftops breaking the canopy of trees here and there. I rented a car, found an economical hotel downtown, and started to look around. Atlanta was one of the most beautiful cities I'd ever seen, with well-manicured lawns and gardens, beautiful trees and interesting neighborhoods.

My search started with the "for rent" ads in the local newspaper, the Atlanta Journal-Constitution. I marked the ones that looked promising and made some calls. But after a day of appointments, I realized I didn't want to live in an apartment building surrounded by other tenants. I wanted a place in a residential neighborhood, maybe a duplex or a small garden apartment. Even more importantly, I wanted to be faithful to the inner wisdom that felt like it was calling me to move to Atlanta. This meant that I didn't want to just look in the newspaper and mechanically respond to ads that met my criteria. So late on Friday afternoon, I asked myself: *What is the place I should be looking for?*

The answer that came shocked me. In my mind's eye, I saw a vivid, fully detailed picture of the exterior of a house. It was a gray, two-story wood house with white trim around the windows. It had a covered porch supported with square wooden pillars across the entire front of the house. The entrance to the downstairs was in the middle of the porch, and the door to the upstairs apartment that I somehow knew was for rent was on the far right. The house was on a small hill rising from the street, with a longer stairway from the street to the top of the hill and a shorter stairway from there up to the front porch. Altogether, the vision had over twenty specific details that made that house unmistakably recognizable – if, somehow, I was able to find it.

Because unfortunately, the image didn't come with an address, and the task of finding that specific house seemed virtually impossible. I felt more than a little frustrated. But the image was so remarkably detailed and vivid that I had to trust that the house was there to be found. I decided to keep looking at the newspaper and real estate rental advertisements, narrow it down to duplexes in residential neighborhoods, and keep searching. I could also speed up the process by driving by places that had addresses. So on Friday evening and all day Saturday, I drove by several dozen prospects, looking for my gray wooden house with white trim around the windows. No luck.

Early Sunday morning, after driving by a few more places that had no resemblance at all to my gray house, something in me just gave up. This was going nowhere, and I was exhausted and discouraged. I also was running out of time. I decided I had to be practical and look at other options. But I was so tired. I went back to my hotel and took a nap.

An hour later, I woke up feeling woozy. I needed a walk to get some fresh air and wake myself up, so I took the elevator down to the street. On Sunday, that part of downtown Atlanta was almost deserted. As I walked around the block, I dimly realized I still needed to find new places to check out, so I picked up a free alternative newspaper from a metal box on the street. Back to my room, I was disappointed to discover that the "for rent" section was only about half a page. But there seemed to be three possibilities that were at least in the ballpark, and I circled them with my pen.

The first one seemed most promising, and it had an address. I drove by, and it looked perfect: a single unit in a modern triplex, with convenient parking and not far from an interesting neighborhood center. Nothing like what I had seen in my mind, but clearly a good place to live. I called the number in the ad, and the owner told me I could see it, but I had to wait until 3:00, which was in about two hours. No problem, I needed to eat lunch anyway.

At 3:00, I was sitting in the parking lot at the triplex, waiting for the owner. At 3:30, I drove to a pay phone and called him, but got no answer. Every few minutes, I called again. Finally, just before 4:00, the owner picked up. "I'm sorry," he said. "It's just been rented."

I felt like my ship was sinking, and sinking fast. What to do? I still had the free newspaper with me, and I looked at the other two ads I'd circled. One of them, I had to wonder what I'd been thinking because it didn't fit what I was looking for at all. The other one might be a possibility, so I called the number.

The woman who answered was in a rush. She was on her way out the door, could I call back later? I said I was in a rush, too, and running out of time to find a place to live. The address she gave me wasn't far away, and I could be there in two minutes. Could come by right now, before she left? She agreed to wait for me.

As I drove up, I realized immediately that I'd found it. The gray house with white trim around the windows, the full porch with square pillars, the second-floor apartment with the entry on the right. She took me upstairs to see the apartment, but I knew it would be fine, and it was. Feeling an excitement I could barely hide, I said I'd take it.

Then she dropped another bombshell. "I've already said I'd rent it to someone else who wants to take a final look at it this evening at 8:00 before deciding," she said. "What do you want to do?"

I said I'd call her at 8:15 and if her other prospect didn't want it, I'd sign a lease. She said that would work and went off to do her errands.

I went back to my hotel, confused. What if the other person rented the apartment? I bought another newspaper and started to look through the rental ads, but then put it down. I'd already found the place where I was supposed to live. I had to trust that if my inner wisdom had gone to such lengths to identify it for me, it had to be available. If I didn't find an apartment before I had to leave town, so be it.

At 8:15, I was sitting in my car in the hardware store parking lot at the end of the street where my house was, staring at a pay phone. I was so anxious, I couldn't bring myself to make the call. A few more minutes went by. Finally, at 8:20, I called the number and tentatively asked whether the apartment was still available.

"Well, the strangest thing happened," she said. "The guy came by and kind of ran through the apartment, mumbled something, and then left. If you'd like to rent it, it's yours."

I ran back to my car and was at my new landlady's door about a minute later. As I was signing the lease, another person rang her doorbell and inquired about the apartment. But the deal was done. I walked down to my car absolutely amazed and thrilled, enormously grateful – and marveling at how it had happened.

Other times and places

Finding that apartment in Atlanta felt like a blessing, an affirmation of my decision to move, and a profound validation of my inner process of discernment. What I decided then, and what I still believe is true, is that finding an apartment in that way was a lesson about the importance of deeply trusting my inner wisdom.

I had to stop thrashing around and "trust myself to the water," as Alan Watts said. When I did, it let me float.

I suspect that the vividness of my inner vision at that time was partly the result of my intensive meditation and spiritual practice, which had helped me unclutter my inner awareness. In addition, the amazing level of detail in my vision of the gray house taught me something about the extraordinary potential for this process. My inner wisdom, which had offered clear but more subtle guidance up to that point, was saying: this is what can happen if you care enough to engage deeply with your life, ask for what you want, pay attention to what your inner wisdom tells you, and trust that you can find it.

As it turned out, this was a perfect apartment for me to start my time in Atlanta. My landlady and her husband became good friends and helped me get oriented to the city. The second-floor apartment itself had six rooms and many charming elements, including a bedroom with windows on three sides that opened into a tree that blossomed gloriously in the Spring. It was close to shops and restaurants, and in an interesting part of town. I enjoyed several years there.

Since then, whenever I've moved from one place to another, I've asked my inner wisdom for an image of the best place for me to live. I've never received anything like the same extraordinary image that I did for that apartment, but about half the time I get at least a few specific visual details that confirm that I've found the place I'm meant to be. When I don't get an image, it usually means that I'm emotionally upset or distracted by something going on in my life that makes it hard to feel clear about the move.

But when I'm inwardly open and available, my inner wisdom shows me some remarkable things. The blue-gray color and architectural details of a single-story Craftsman-style house I bought with a friend in Atlanta. A specific bit of stonework on the façade that identified an apartment I rented in Chicago. The image of a square brown house with a lovely attic apartment in Rochester, New York that I rented when I arrived for graduate school. The broken downstairs white porch rail of a second-floor apartment in Rochester that became one of my all-time favorite places to live. The image of a garden right outside the apartment I rented when I came to Chicago to take my first job as a psychologist, with its distinctly shaped wood border and small, red flowers planted about eighteen inches apart.

One other story about finding a place to live is worth telling for the lesson I learned from it. About a dozen years after the extraordinary experience of finding an apartment in Atlanta, I'd completed my graduate work and was moving to Chicago for a health psychology internship. I decided to move to the western suburb of Oak Park, which was a short commute to my internship at Rush Medical Center on Chicago's West Side. This time, I didn't have the luxury of apartment shopping for an entire weekend. With a tight schedule, I had to find an apartment in a single day. In fact, I wanted to finish early enough in the day so I could drive up to Milwaukee and have dinner with my friend Steve and his family. I chose a rental agent with a non-profit organization that had a good reputation for promoting housing diversity in Oak Park, and made an appointment to see apartments at 11:00 a.m. I prayerfully asked for the first one I saw to be right for me, and then looked within for insight about it.

What came to me was strange. I got an image of a semicircular building with a curved roof like a Quonset hut, with a single door in the middle and windows on each side. There was pavement right up to the edge of the building. All of this was puzzling, and it didn't look even remotely like an apartment. But I showed up, hopeful, for my 11:00 a.m. appointment with the rental agent.

The first apartment she took me to see was in a lovely old brownstone, on the second floor, that had been rented by an elderly woman for the previous thirty years. It had beautiful dark oak interior trim, hardwood floors, and a semi-modern kitchen. It was something of a mess, since the long-time tenant had kept the windows open so she could feed the neighborhood squirrels inside the apartment. But the building owners were cleaning it out and painting it, it had beautiful woodwork, and it was relatively cheap. What did I think?

Well, it was perfect. But where was the curved roof and the pavement right up to the edge of the building? We went on to the next two apartments, neither of which was anywhere near as interesting as the first. Did she have any more to look at? She reminded me that their policy was to only show three apartments at a time. She dropped me off at the rental agency and went on to her next appointment.

I was disappointed that my inner wisdom seemed to have failed me. I still had to find a place to live, so I bought a local newspaper and sat in a coffee shop, looking at the rental ads. Then I put the newspaper down. No, this wasn't right. I had to be missing something. I drove back to the first apartment and took another look.

The outside of the building hadn't changed since I'd been there an hour earlier. It was still a conventional-looking brownstone, still beautiful. Nothing about it seemed curved at all. Maybe I should rent it anyway? Then I remembered the rental agent had said that parking for the building was around the side and in back, and I hadn't checked it out. I walked around the side of the building.

As I turned the corner, I found myself facing the back of an auto parts and repair shop in an old curved-roof Quonset hut. Parking spaces on the pavement went right up to the edge of the building, which had a door in the middle and windows on each side, exactly as I'd seen it in my mind. It was unmistakably the unique cue I was given to identify that apartment, and I was amazed and delighted. Furthermore, just as I'd asked, it had been the first building I looked at, and I still had time to go see Steve and his family for dinner. I drove back to the rental agency to fill out the paperwork, knowing that my trust in inner wisdom had been affirmed yet again.

What it means

I do not want to claim too much, or too little, for these experiences. They were certainly more detailed than what most people experience from their inner wisdom – and more than I do, too, most of the time. I don't experience visions every day, or even every year. The incredibly detailed and vivid image I received of the gray frame house with white trim was, I suspect, a once-in-a-lifetime experience. It also is quite extraordinary that the images of places to live that I've seen were so specific and accurate, and beyond any information I had at the time I received them. How this could happen is beyond what I can explain, but it points toward a remarkable fact: our inner wisdom connects us with information that we do not already know. How amazing is that! I believe that this is direct experiential evidence that we are connected with each other and with the world in ways that transcend our ordinary biological and physical understanding of ourselves.

I also think it's possible to say something about what inspires inner wisdom to show up, and perhaps what its purpose might be. The ordinary or extraordinary insight and information that inner wisdom offers appears to be in response to genuine human needs. But it's not there as neutral data of the sort that you might access with an internet search engine or by opening a book. It seems to be tailored specifically to who you are, where you are on your life's journey, what your thoughts, beliefs, feelings and psychological issues allow you to be aware of, your ability to access your deeper inner states of being, and what you truly want and need. In other words, it's not just about getting what you're asking for in the moment. The insight from your inner wisdom is coming from a bigger place than your own desires, and takes into account what you need to grow as a person.

For me, a significant part of my personal growth around the experience of inner wisdom has been to learn to trust the process. My somewhat unusual willingness to make life-changing decisions to follow my inner promptings is certainly one of the personal traits or gifts that allowed me to explore this as deeply as I have. Nonetheless, early on when I had less experience with it, I often felt conflicted and doubtful about the process.

Having grown from and set aside my own doubts and fears, I'm optimistic that others can do so, too. If you take on this challenge, it becomes part of your human journey to learn to trust your inner wisdom when you're faced with important questions, issues, and situations. The risk you take when you do is that you sometimes make decisions that initially look a bit strange to others, and even to yourself. The benefit is that by cultivating and trusting your inner wisdom, you can be confident that the path you follow in life is truly yours.

I wrote this poem in Atlanta, during a time when I was making profound personal changes and coming to new realizations about myself. At the heart of those changes was learning to trust my true self and bring my life into alignment with the deepest truth I knew.

EVOLUTION

1.

Asleep, the twig breaks.
On the hillside, water
makes trails in the dust.

The old monk realizes
he must start over.

Solitude, without even himself.
The flame on his candle
does not touch the wick.

2.

Silence illuminates the night.
Moleskin, tiny paws
moving through earth.

What is invisible is so clear!

There's no need to approach
what is already here.

3.

On the hillside,
a thousand blossoms
turn toward the sun.

The old monk
laughs out loud.

Can it be so easy?
Every flower in the field
can count to One.

Chapter 3
Courage

Life shrinks or expands in proportion to one's courage.

– Anaïs Nin

While I was living in Atlanta in the early and mid-1980s, the AIDS epidemic began. Originally and incorrectly labelled a "gay disease," it had a terrifying mortality rate. With no effective treatment for several years (antiviral medicines didn't become available until 1987), close to 100% of people infected with the HIV virus died. People with AIDS (a person with AIDS was respectfully called a PWA) were stigmatized and shunned, and there was general fear in the community about being around them since there were questions about how the virus was transmitted. It was recognized early on that sexual activity and blood-to-blood contact could lead to infection, but what if you touched something a PWA had touched or were around someone who sneezed? We know now that casual contact like this can't transmit the virus, but it was still a question that people were uncertain about in the early years of the disease.

Around the same time, I was starting to explore bringing a healing intention into my interactions with others. My friend

Jerry Epps had moved to Atlanta after a few years in Tucson, and offered a class for people who wanted to learn how to do a simple form of spiritual healing or "energy work," as it's sometimes called, that he developed by combining practices from several healing traditions.

He and I were both quite busy and had a hard time getting together, so the thought came to me that if I took his class, I could spend some time with him and we could occasionally go out for coffee afterwards. In retrospect, I'm sure that this excuse to take his class was a prompt from my inner wisdom to learn what he was teaching. My first experience with energy healing was a revelation: it felt just like the inner experience of energy when I did t'ai chi! I found this fascinating. People on the receiving end told me they felt a warmth or tingling from my hands even though I wasn't physically touching them. They were relaxed and comforted, and sometimes had less pain. That clinched it for me. Cultivating a healing relationship with people was deeply meaningful to me, and I wanted to do more of this intriguing work. After completing Jerry's class, I joined a year-long training program he created for people who wanted to become healing ministers.

After six months of practice with other people in the class (in every session it seemed we had an interesting experience or learned something new), the healing minister training program involved us in a six-month community practicum. I felt drawn to volunteer with people with AIDS. PWAs often had little energy for household tasks or anything else, and just having someone come in to wash dishes or do a few loads of laundry was helpful.

So, working through an AIDS volunteer organization, I did those simple but useful things for them. Once I met and got to know the people I was helping, I also offered the energy healing I was learning to do. I described it as something that was comforting and sometimes helpful at reducing physical discomfort and pain. I said that it might also have a positive effect on their health, although that was certainly not a sure thing. Every person I offered the energy work to accepted it. Most reported at least some measure of comfort and relief from their symptoms, sometimes even from symptoms as severe as the bouts of uncontrollable sweating that PWAs periodically experienced.

After my first couple of home visits, though, despite my inner guidance to do this work, I started to wonder if I was putting my life at risk. The information I'd heard at that time about how one might get infected with HIV hadn't made it clear whether I was safe being around PWAs if they coughed or sneezed. I also wasn't clear about whether it was safe to clean the dishes I was washing or handle the clothes I touched when I did laundry because at the time I had a nervous habit of chewing the skin on the side of my fingernails, which sometimes led to open sores. I became worried that I might become infected. The question came to me: Was I willing to lose my life to do this work?

Perhaps strangely, despite my worry, the logical and obvious answer of "no" didn't seem right to me. After sitting with the question for several days, I realized that the truth inside me was actually "Yes." I was in fact willing to lose my life to do volunteer work with people who so desperately needed help. I would be as careful as I reasonably could, but if my work in service to others cost me my life, so be it.

This was a level of commitment to serving others that I'd never made before, and something inside me shifted profoundly when I made that decision. At that moment, my inner wisdom let me know that I would not die from being an AIDS volunteer. In fact, it let me know how long I would live. I felt reassured and encouraged by this insight, and felt that I could take reasonable risks in service to others without being concerned about dying prematurely. That inner knowing is certainly one of the greatest gifts I've ever received. In the years since then, I've been confidently able to follow what I'm led to do as a health psychologist and a volunteer without worrying about losing my life.

The courage to be who you are

Finding the courage to follow your subtle inner promptings is difficult, and one of the most counter-cultural things you'll ever do. It's usually not about the physical risks you might experience, though. It's more likely to be about having the courage to follow through on your inner wisdom even when it places you at odds with the expectations of the people around you – and perhaps your own. Over and over in my work as a psychologist, I've been saddened by how often people feel that they have to be silent about their own truth or give it up because of the demands or judgments of other people in their life or how they might look.

I have dealt with this challenge in my life, too. When I was growing up, my parents, who were of an older generation, didn't want to hear my personal thoughts and feelings. The cliché that "children should be seen and not heard" was a reality for me. I had to remain silent about what was going on inside me except for ten minutes during the week that my mom designated as "talking time." That constraint had a paralyzing and negative effect on me for many years. It kept me from speaking up about what I felt or really wanted, or at times even being aware of it. In my teen years, my fear and lack of confidence in what I cared about were so real to me that they controlled and limited my relationships and the activities I let myself be involved with. Even soccer and astronomy, which I loved, weren't "serious" enough activities for me to spend time on during my first years in college. When I finally found the clarity and courage to bring those activities back into my life, things started to turn around for me.

As I know from my own life, the demands, expectations, and judgments of other people can be crippling. These external pressures can lead you to accumulate defenses like a sea creature's shell. You might design your shell to get the support and approval of others, as I did early on, and it may be successful or even beautiful, in its way – but its primary purpose is to create a defensive barrier. A shell of silence, false responses, compromises, and misdirection defends you against the demands of others.

At its worst, you may be hiding inside your shell because you've suffered emotional, physical or sexual abuse and not been able to speak up about it – or because you've had to force yourself into a career, a marriage or some other major life choice you didn't want that others pressured you to pursue. Sadly, if that happens, the choices you have may feel as limited as those a parent gives a child at dinnertime: Would you like broccoli or spinach? Without finding the courage to stand up for what's true for you, what you really like and care about no longer even makes the list, and you end up feeling trapped and lost.

Resisting distraction, judgment and separation

The challenge of staying aware of your inner wisdom and who you really are requires you to deal with more than your emotional wounds and defenses, however. You also face it when you encounter everyday social and cultural experiences, which requires its own sort of courage to resist. There are distractions from electronic media, popular magazines, television shows, the news, and the increasingly commercial world of vendors with ulterior motives and fellow consumers with artificially stimulated appetites. Being preoccupied by entertainment, celebrities, social media and sports can feel exciting, and your frustration and anger about politics and scandals can be addicting, but it separates you from your inner wisdom.

Courage is also needed to stand up for the deepest truth you know is when you're involved in the intellectual life of the mind. At its best, the intellectual world can be rich, illuminating, and persuasive – but it can also be judgmental and dismissive of phenomena outside its conceptual boundaries. For those drawn to it (and I was one of those people for a long time), the analytic assumptions of the academic and scientific world can lead to the belief that an intellectual understanding is all you need to know about anything. But the process of carefully defining something, analyzing its components and functions, and discovering the complex relationships it has with what's around it isn't particularly useful when you try to discern a deep personal truth. In my view, it's impossible to think your way into an exclusively intellectual understanding of a personally important question. Should I marry that special person? Is this the right career for me? Does God exist? Your intellectual understanding of what truly matters to you is always limited, and it takes courage to look deeper for answers to questions that are personally meaningful. The deepest truth you know is more elusive to intellectual inquiry than the center of the earth.

It's necessary to courageously resist other ways of thinking can also keep you from your inner wisdom, too. For example, a regular practice of black-and-white, critical, or judgmental thinking is quite likely to make you believe that you're in touch with "the truth." It's a heady experience when you think you're right about something – or everything. It's easy to build your sense of self, your relationships, or even your career around the things you're absolutely certain that you're right about and others are wrong about. It is particularly difficult to resist if you've surrounded yourself with others who think in the same way. A well-rationalized practice of judging, dividing, condemning – or even approving – the world around you throws a blanket over your experiences so you no longer see, hear, understand and feel them directly. It has a particularly corrosive effect on relationships. Far from leading you toward the deepest truth you know, filling your world with righteous judgments and dogmatic analyses of others keeps you from directly experiencing those people and can destroy your closest relationships.

When you don't stand up against these dismissive judgments in yourself, the consequences can be tragic. A young man I knew back in the 1980s was one of the first people in Atlanta to contract AIDS. He was homosexual and estranged from his conservative Christian parents because they judged his sexual orientation to be sinful. But after he was diagnosed with AIDS, his parents agreed to go through counseling with him so they could try to understand each other better and perhaps reestablish their relationship before he died, which was the expected medical outcome at that time. After an entire year of counseling and talking about their lives, however, his parents decided that if he wasn't going to change his sexual orientation, they would break off all contact with him. He was profoundly shocked at their lack of understanding and their unwillingness to look beyond the dictates of their religion to see him as a person – and to love him as their son. He died a few months later, still grieving the loss of his family but, thankfully, surrounded by friends who loved him.

Even the idea that there is a way to live the deepest truth you know contains subtle seeds of judgment and separation that need to be courageously resisted – particularly by me. Before I started writing this book, I attended a week-long workshop with a remarkable spiritual teacher I've admired for many years, Dr. Richard Moss. When I told Richard that I intended to write a book called *Living the Deepest Truth You Know*, he said, "When I heard your title, I was afraid that it would lead to suffering." His insight was a wonderful gift. It wouldn't be hard for me to divide up the world into "the people who live their deepest truth" and "the people who don't," or to judge them on how well they live their deepest truth.

That is surely not what I want to do, or what I intend this book to do. Learning how to live your deepest truth is a unique and personal journey. Everyone has their own version of the barriers to inner wisdom that I've outlined above, and no one deals with them perfectly, including me. Please be gentle with yourself as you do the difficult work of setting aside the habits and ways of thinking that separate you from your inner wisdom. Like all of us, you start with your own challenges and gifts, and courageously accepting yourself as you are is the first step in learning how to open to the deepest truth you know.

Positive thoughts, beliefs and values

There's also another, more subtle challenge to inner wisdom: your positive thoughts and beliefs about who you are and what you most value and love. Suppose you've closely examined your life experience and engaged in practices that have helped you grow personally and spiritually. As a result, maybe you've cultivated positive personal qualities such as acceptance, patience, compassion, kindness, and love for others. Perhaps you've developed positive beliefs about what is true and good about yourself, the people you love, what it is to be healthy, or how to understand God. Or you've learned ways to understand and relate to people who are different than you or difficult to deal with, and how to be compassionate and kind to them. Or you've been inspired by and embraced social justice issues, and have learned how to speak up and take action to make the world a better place. Surely those positive beliefs and actions must matter as you explore your deepest truth?

Well, of course they matter. Your most positive and enlightened thoughts and beliefs about yourself, others, the world, religion, and spirituality should rightly play an important role in your life. Even so, there's an interesting paradox: your positive, compassionate and loving beliefs and values may be the foundation for your life and your understanding of the world, but they are not the specific and unique experience of the deepest truth you know. As Buddhists say, your finger pointing to the moon is not the moon, and you are at risk of missing the moon (a deeper truth) if you look only at your finger (your thoughts or beliefs about that truth). Your deepest truth, in whatever situation you find yourself, will not arise if you simply recite your beliefs or engage in rote actions based on them.

Remember that becoming aware of your deepest truth requires you to open yourself to where it lives in the fertile ground of the present moment. This often requires courage, particularly to make the choice to hold your most cherished thoughts, beliefs, and values gently enough to see a deeper truth about the situation or the people involved in it. When you take that brave and perhaps difficult step, your inner wisdom may show you a deeper truth than your usual thoughts and beliefs, even your positive ones. Your inner wisdom may offer a different way of seeing a situation or a person, suggest setting aside judgments that you may be making, or ask you to consider additional aspects of the situation or person that you hadn't been thinking about. It may even ask you to think differently about yourself.

There are also times when you'll find a constructive interaction between inner wisdom and your values and beliefs. In addition to offering its own unique and different perspective, inner wisdom can also guide you to see how your positive values and beliefs apply to the specific circumstance you find yourself in. For example, one of my good friends was dealing with stressful relationships in her family. Somewhat despairingly, she said, "Well, I guess I just need to remember that I'm God's daughter." The sadness on her face and the resignation in her voice, though, made it clear that her positive belief wasn't enough to reassure and comfort her.

OK, I said. That's a good place to start. But how does that deep truth apply to what's going on with you right now?

Her face brightened immediately. "Oh!" she said. "It means that I don't need to carry this by myself. I can turn it over to God."

That insight about how her positive beliefs applied to her deepest truth of the present moment let her see her situation with different eyes and respond to it with a different heart.

A young person's courage

Another example of the deepest truth you know arising courageously in the moment came from my fellow Circle of Trust facilitator, Lori. She grew up in a family with, as she put it, "a big sense of justice." Her father was a police officer in Washington D.C. during the riots of the 1960s. At the same time, her family was very open-hearted, and had people of all sorts in and out of their house. Everybody was welcome. With so many people around, she discovered that, like her grandmother, she often had an intuitive sense about them. She also remembered her father telling her that if she listened to herself closely enough, she would always know the right thing to do.

"I think those experiences allowed me to stay connected to that deep inner place in myself where I knew between right and wrong," she said. "It's the way I was raised and the values I was given, for sure. But part of it was staying connected to the core of who I am, and always listening to the important voices rising up within me."

When she was in the sixth grade, Lori had a physical education teacher who seemed pretty cool on the surface but treated the pretty girls and athletic boys differently than the other kids. "This felt like an injustice to me," she said, "even though I might not have used that word as a sixth grader."

She remembers one classmate in particular who was treated badly because she was physically awkward, taller than everyone and very thin. She also had orthodontic headgear that circled her head, and she wore glasses. "But she was really a lovely person and I sensed that it wasn't right how other people treated her."

Lori and her class were out on the field one day. It was football season and they were doing "down and outs" where they would run, turn around when they reached a cone, and then catch a ball that the physical education teacher passed to them. When it was her classmate's turn, she ran down awkwardly and missed the ball. The teacher made her stand at the cone in front of everybody to embarrass her.

Lori leaned toward me. "That was the first time that I could very loudly and clearly hear my inner voice saying, *You have to say something. This is not right. I don't care that he's an adult. If the ball hits her face she could break her nose, it will hurt her.*"

She did speak up to the teacher, right there in the middle of the field. "I don't remember exactly what I said, but it was something to the effect of, 'Why are you doing this? You know she can get hurt. You know she wears braces and glasses. Other people are going to miss the ball, why are you picking on her? You're acting like a bully.'

"Of course, he dismissed what I said," said Lori. But she told the principal what had happened, and told her parents, and her parents called her classmate's parents, and the next year that teacher was not rehired. "That's when I realized, OK, I know I heard that loud and clear, and I was true to it."

The way Lori understood what was right was the result of her family's positive values of acceptance, justice and fairness. But by itself, what you understand and believe is never enough. In that moment on the playground, the courage to speak up and act arose from her willingness to listen to and respond to her inner wisdom. She had to look past the assumptions and pressures of the social situation she was in, which would have kept her silent about the actions of a person in authority, her teacher. By being true to the deepest truth she knew, however, she had the courage to confront her teacher, and then take meaningful action with the school principal and her parents to change how her friend was treated. Lori learned from that experience that by acting on the deepest truth she knows, she can make a positive difference in the world.

Turning toward your truth

If you're like many people, your journey to follow the deepest truth you know might be starting later in life. The decision to begin that journey when your life seems settled is particularly difficult and takes its own kind of courage. Suppose that after years or even decades of ignoring the gentle promptings of your inner wisdom, you start paying attention to them. It might be quite painful to identify and change the places in your life where you're not being true to yourself. A life built on something other than your deepest truth is going to be shaken up when you start paying attention to your inner wisdom and acting on it. Things may seem temporarily worse as you let go of the people and activities that aren't true for you and turn to those that are.

Doing this may be the greatest challenge of your life. You might be in a prestigious and lucrative career that means nothing personal to you, or in a loveless relationship that's stable and financially secure. Or you may have expectations about the lifestyle you think you're supposed to live (or entitled to live) that make any alternatives seem impossible. There's too much at risk, you might think, too much you'd lose, too many people who might be disappointed, angry or hurt – yourself included. You may well be the person with the most rigid expectations about who you are and what you do, and have the greatest stake in keeping things the way they are. When the still, small voice of truth starts to speak to you, your first impulse may be to tell it to shut up.

I know from sad personal experience what it's like to silence my inner wisdom. Even after I started to be aware of a deeper truth in my own life, I sometimes ignored it – and I deeply regret doing so. In my work, relationships, and personal life, I have made decisions based on money, desire, insecurity, or fear that I knew weren't right even as I made them. As I review them in my mind, I realize that every one of those choices (let me repeat: *every one*) resulted in something less than I thought it would. Some of them led to agonizing personal failures, missed opportunities, lawsuits, financial problems, other people being hurt, and the loss of love and friendship.

What I learned from those experiences is that in the midst of my most emotionally involved and distracted moments, I need to hit the pause button. I need to stop what I'm doing and create the space and intention to be aware of my inner wisdom. I also need to be brave enough to take my inner wisdom seriously even when – *especially* when – I'm tempted by outward success or reluctant to follow it because of my ego's concerns. Thankfully, it's always there if I'm willing to listen, no matter how far I may have drifted away from it.

It's there for you, too. Your wise inner knowing is trying to speak to you, even through your distractions, guilt, depression, and pain. The challenge is to find the trust and courage to make your way through the hurts and conditioning of your past, as well as the temptations of the present, and let your inner wisdom be the heart of who you are and what you do.

I've written several long poems about my parents. This shorter one reflects a hard-won inner reconciliation with them that I found after years of therapy and in my connection with them through nature. It was evoked by a painting I encountered in an art gallery.

EVENING LAKE

I've seen this lake all my life
in dreams, and in my travels
off the map, up north.

It is the lake where my father
and I went fishing in the quiet evening,
the lake where my mother fished
at dawn before anyone else
was awake.

It is the lake where my father
taught me how to kill an animal
when I had to,
the lake where my mother
taught me how to cry
without showing it.

It is the lake where I lost them both
to anger and grief –
and it is the lake where, years later,
I found them again.

It is the lake I go to
when all else fails.

– Inspired by the painting
Evening Lake, by William Buxton

Chapter 4
Asking for Your Truth

Ask and it will be given to you; seek, and you will find; knock, and the door will be opened to you.

– Matthew 7:7, *NIV*

A few months after I started to think seriously about making the process of living the deepest truth you know a greater part of my life and work, I had a counseling session with a client named Elsa. She was an elderly woman in her mid-80s with heart disease who I had been meeting with for several months. In addition to her heart troubles, she was suffering from the fact that she had not spoken with her nearly 60-year-old son for over 30 years. They had briefly acknowledged each other at family gatherings, and she had written many letters and tried in other ways to communicate, but her son hadn't responded.

Then after Elsa had her second heart attack, her son wrote her a note and said he wanted to talk. At this point in her life, though, Elsa wasn't sure she wanted to reopen the relationship. There had been so much hurt and disappointment, she was afraid that reconnecting with him was going to reopen old wounds and create new pain. Out of fear, she kept her son at a distance for several months. "I want to end my life in peace," she told me. "I can't talk to him if all he's going to do is hurt me again."

After we talked about what she was afraid he might do or say, we reached a moment where we seemed to be waiting for what would come next. So I asked, "What's the deepest truth you know about your son?"

She was quiet for a moment, then said, "All I can see is this happy little eight-year-old boy coming in the back door of our home the way he used to, and shouting, 'Honey, I'm home!'"

We both smiled. "If that's the deepest truth you know about your son," I said, "how do you feel about meeting with him?"

With that nonthreatening and joyful image in her mind, Elsa was able to meet with her son and talk about what had kept them apart. Conversation between them wasn't easy, and she was still afraid of discovering what he might be blaming her for. But the insight about her son opened the door between them. Progress in their relationship became possible after she was willing to look beyond her fear and follow the deepest truth she knew.

Asking for the deepest truth you know

"What's the deepest truth you know?" is not a question that's usually asked in psychotherapy – or at other times. However, as I thought about how inner wisdom sometimes works to provide insight in the murky confusion of a personal crisis, it reminded me of the situations facing many of the people I saw as psychotherapy clients. I began to wonder what would happen if I asked clients to shift attention away from their overwhelming feelings or confusing thoughts by directly asking them for the deepest truth they knew about their troubling situations.

I thought carefully about when I might ask that question and what clients it might and might not be appropriate for. The potential to promote insight and growth seemed promising, though, and worth trying. The first client I asked that question to was

Elsa, and her positive response got me thinking about the possibilities and benefits of taking a more direct route to the deepest truth you know.

The deepest truth you know shows up in two ways. As I started to become aware of and respond to my inner wisdom when I was younger, sometimes I received guidance that arose spontaneously out of my general situation. The insights that came to me about finding time to write and moving to Kansas City and Atlanta, the desire to learn t'ai chi, the not-very-logical idea of going back to school to get a master's degree in psychology so I could get a better part-time job, and many others seemed to arise without my directly asking for them. My inner wisdom came forward in situations when I needed it, even if I didn't know that I did.

The other way I've been guided is when I've directly asked for it, such as when I asked for insight about places to live. Many other people have done this, too. The story in the first chapter of Elizabeth Gilbert on her bathroom floor, begging for an answer to the question of what she should do next with her life, is an example of asking explicitly for inner wisdom. I've also seen people receive insight about questions or issues that they were addressing during activities specifically designed to facilitate access to inner wisdom, such as Circle of Trust® retreats and Clearness Committees, which I'll describe later.

My favorite example, though, is my wife Laurin. As I described in the introduction, she simply started acting on the statement I made in our living room: "Find the deepest truth you know and let everything else fall in place around it." By asking for the deepest truth she knows and making the commitment to let other considerations fall in place around it, she regularly receives insight and guidance on handling challenging situations. Asking directly for her deepest truth helps her find the way forward in her life. Most recently, this process led her to go back to school to get an MFA in creative writing.

I've found something both humbling and exhilarating about asking directly for my inner wisdom. It's humbling because I am always conscious that my inner wisdom is offering me something beyond my own human awareness and understanding, such as when I'm looking for a place to live. Yet it's always respectful of my needs and limitations. It gives me guidance when I've asked to find a place to live in a certain area or neighborhood that was convenient or appealing. It's respected my financial limitations when I've had to carefully define a range of rents I could afford. (Interestingly, my inner wisdom has nearly always guided me to apartments or houses near the top end of my budget!) As I've described earlier, I often had a time constraint and needed an answer within a few days or even hours. I find it amazing that somehow my inner wisdom has been able to guide me to what I needed, even with my personal limitations and circumstances.

Looking back, there's one additional factor that I didn't see then but am grateful for now. Whether I received guidance spontaneously or deliberately asked for it, I never questioned whether I was worthy of receiving it. It simply came to me with a deep sense of personal truth. I didn't struggle with self-doubting questions about where the guidance was coming from, and I didn't agonize over whether I deserved to accept the opportunities that my insight opened up for me. My inner wisdom was in sync with my self-esteem as well as my life situation, and never suggested something I couldn't follow through on, emotionally or financially. As a result, I was always able to trust and feel confident in the insight I received, even when it challenged me to stretch beyond where I was.

Making inner connections

The experience with Elsa went so well that a few weeks later, I tried suggesting to another client that he ask for the deepest truth he knew.

Pastor Sam was an older minister with a problem: he couldn't seem to retire. He was in his early seventies and had been an Episcopalian minister all his adult life. He had now retired from three different churches, but after each retirement he felt so depressed that he immediately looked for another place to preach.

Ten years earlier, he'd had the very painful experience of leaving a congregation when it was clear that many of the church leaders didn't want him to stay. "That was my first 'retirement' from ministry," he said. "It was so painful. For a minister to be asked to leave is like being separated from part of your soul." Nonetheless, he had handled his departure well, with a minimum of divisiveness in the congregation.

The most painful thing in his life, however, was the death of his son, which occurred about two years before he was asked to leave that church. "I think of him every day," he said. "No one ever gets over the death of a child."

We had talked over these issues and others in his life for several sessions, and I asked him what he thought about when he remembered his departure from the church. "I think about the sense of betrayal I had when two of the church council leaders started to oppose me," he said. In our session, I had him use a technique to reduce some of his distress around that experience, and he felt his emotional pain lessen after a few minutes.

Then I asked Pastor Sam for the deepest truth he knew about his departure from that church. "You mean the sense of betrayal?" he asked.

Is that the deepest truth you know about it? I asked.

"Do you mean how upset I felt, how lost I felt?"

Is that the deepest truth you know? I repeated.

He was quiet for a few moments. "That was such a hard time," he said. "My son died two years before all that happened. It hurt so much. I went to two memorial services for him out of town in the places he had grown up and had friends, and then the next week, I had to be back in the pulpit at my church. My congregation wanted a memorial service to say farewell to him and comfort me and my wife, but I couldn't bear to go through another one. So we had a reception where people could come up to me and talk. But I never could stand in front of the church and talk about the death of my son."

Did you ever really share with your church family what you were going through?

"No," he said. "I think congregations want to see their minister as strong, not vulnerable to having those things happen in their lives. And they started to feel distant from me when it happened."

Maybe, I said gently, that's how you wanted to see yourself, too, as strong. But not talking about what you were going through, do you think that may have created some separation between yourself and your congregation?

Pastor Sam thought for a moment, and his eyes became sad. "Yes," he said, almost in a whisper. "I see that."

Perhaps you and your congregation started to move apart from each other when you couldn't share the most difficult experience of your life. What do you think about going back, even now, ten years later, and giving a sermon about the loss of your son?

He was silent for a moment. "I'll pray about that," he said.

As Pastor Sam tried to respond to my initial question about the deepest truth he knew about his departure from that church, he was quite understandably drawn to thinking about his feelings of betrayal and distress. Until he was able to set those feelings aside and let the loss of his son enter his awareness in an unexpected way, he was unable to see a connection between his forced departure from his church and the distance he had created with his congregation around his grief.

In retrospect, I regret making the suggestion that Pastor Sam give a sermon on the loss of his son. Instead, with what I know

now about creating safe space for inner wisdom, I would have asked a less directive, open-ended question that would have let him to explore what he might do to express and resolve his grief. Thankfully, Pastor Sam was in touch with his own process for accessing his inner wisdom and could put my suggestion in its proper place for his life. After praying about it, he eventually decided *not* to follow my suggestion to go back and give a talk about his son, but he did other things to come to closure around his grief. He was also eventually able to retire comfortably from ministry – as long as he had opportunities to preach as a substitute minister.

My sessions with Pastor Sam and Elsa helped me understand more about the process of asking directly for the deepest truth you know. They clearly showed me that the truth that comes isn't just a rehash of the thoughts and feelings you're mired in. When your sincere and heartfelt questioning finally gets you to your deepest truth, you experience something more than those emotions and thoughts. You may have a sense of mild surprise or of deeper recognition accompanied by a sense of fulfillment or completion. As they both found, when a deep truth reveals itself, there's also often a sense of letting go and affirmation.

Those sessions showed me the transformative power of sincerely asking for the deepest truth you know. Our willingness to listen beyond the easy answers to our human problems can show us new insights and possibilities. But there are limits to the process of asking directly and times when it won't work.

Why asking works – and when it doesn't

When I first experimented with the process of asking directly for the deepest truth you know with Elsa and Pastor Sam, I felt optimistic. I became confident enough to try it with someone I didn't know well who was looking for direction in her life. But when I suggested she ask for the deepest truth she knew about her present life situation, she looked at me strangely.

"That isn't a very good question," she said. "It's unsophisticated." I was a bit shocked – but I shouldn't have been. In her understanding of what I was asking her to look for, she was absolutely right.

What I hadn't taken into account was the supportive, safe and trusting relationships I had developed with Elsa and Pastor Sam in our counseling sessions that made it possible for me to ask them to explore the deepest truth they knew. Your inner wisdom will only be able to respond to "What's the deepest truth you know?" if you feel personally safe and have a context for it to appear in a deep and genuine way. Without that context, someone might assume they should answer by trying to figure out the most rational, advantageous, profitable, acceptable, or agreeable response, or a response that's in line with what they already think or feel. In all of those cases, it is indeed an unsophisticated question.

Even worse, though, the question can be used to trivialize the idea of your "deepest truth," making it ironic, sarcastic or cynical. Or someone might think, "I'm going to call whatever I'd do anyway, 'My Deepest Truth.'" It's also easy to imagine people using the phrase to manipulate others, fervently calling whatever they think or want "the deepest truth I know" so that other people will take their message seriously or do whatever they tell them to do. They might also use it to manipulate themselves into having more confidence in an idea or a person than they should, and dismiss doubts and considerations that should be part of their discernment process.

But suppose you do have an accurate understanding of what the question means and a safe environment for your inner wisdom to respond to it. Why does asking directly work at all? How is it that the question "What's the deepest truth you know?" opens the door for genuine insight?

One possibility is that, assuming you're in a context where you feel safe to respond to it, the question sets an intention and an expectation for you to become aware of your inner wisdom. However, while I'm sure that's an important part of the process, I don't think it's the main story.

There's something unusual that happens when you ask "What's the deepest truth I know about…?" It's quite impossible to respond to this question in a rational, logical, way – and this may be why it works to set aside the easy solutions or answers you might otherwise come up with.

When you ask for the deepest truth you know about a difficult issue or personal challenge, your human, ego-centered self simply doesn't have a way to respond. It gets stuck on what "truth" means and what your "deepest truth" might be about. In a sense, the question acts something like a Zen koan, which is a statement or question containing a paradox that can't be answered rationally. "What is the sound of one hand clapping?" and similar koans are impossible to answer in a literal way. However, in struggling with such a question, a student of Zen might have a sudden intuitive enlightenment about the nature of mind and self that is beyond rational thinking.

Similarly, asking "What's the deepest truth you know?" explicitly throws your ordinary thoughts and feelings against a wall that they can't penetrate. Your bafflement when you ask for the deepest truth you know can allow you to look beyond the thoughts and feelings you already have. Think about Pastor Sam. When I repeatedly asked him for the deepest truth he knew about being asked to leave his former church, he let go of his sense of betrayal, loss and distress and came to a new insight about what was going on. Releasing conventional understanding and emotional control is often a relief because you're letting go of the struggle to understand something you can't rationally figure out. As you let go, you step back from the issue and become quieter inside, which can open you to a deeper insight.

That's not to say that "What's the deepest truth you know?"

has some unique magic that will reveal your inner wisdom better than anything else you might say or do. Nondirective open-ended questions and metaphorical "third things" in Circles of Trust and Clearness Committees, which I'll discuss in the next section, have a similar effect: they nudge you to go beyond your usual way of looking at your question or issue so you can find deeper insight into it. They also have the advantage of not directly confronting and potentially arousing your resistance to new insights. Even a heartfelt and wordless yearning can do this, such as Elizabeth Gilbert's plaintive prayer in her bathroom.

It's clear, however, that in the right circumstances, asking directly for the deepest truth you know can work well. It's also a more effective way to open to your inner wisdom than asking something like, "What is the most loving thing I can say to this person?" or "What is the best way to solve this problem?" or even, if you're a Christian, "What would Jesus do?" When you ask those questions, you already have expectations about loving things to say and your favorite problem-solving strategies, or assumptions about Jesus's behavior, that would let your rational mind think it already knows or can figure out the answer. Questions of that sort, while they may be a positive or constructive way to think, will keep your thoughts in familiar territory and may limit access to a deeper truth.

Circles of Trust and Clearness Committees

As I mentioned earlier, the fact that connecting with inner wisdom isn't limited to being a process of individual contemplation and discernment was a revelation to me. In fact, the idea that the delicate, intimate process of obtaining insight could also happen in a group with other people seemed so improbable that I'd never even thought about it. Despite being a psychologist and having experience with many kinds of therapy and personal growth groups, I had never been in a group where I'd felt it was possible to access that type of insight and inner wisdom until I attended a retreat based on the principles and practices developed by Parker Palmer.

In his book that I mentioned previously, *A Hidden Wholeness*, Parker describes a group process he calls a Circle of Trust® that makes it possible for participants to receive new insight into their lives. Parker is a Quaker and took as part of his model the 370-year-old tradition of Quaker meetings for worship where participants gather in silence and invite spiritual insight from what they call the "inner light" or "inner teacher." Rather than have an explicitly spiritual understanding of the process, though, the Circle of Trust approach simply considers this as opening to your true self or soul, the most authentic part of who you are as a human being.

To do this remarkable thing, the group agrees to specific guidelines or "touchstones" for their interactions to create a positive and safe space where it becomes possible to discover your deepest truth. The touchstones ask you to be welcoming to others in the group, invite participation (not demand it), speak in ways that respect everyone's truth, respect confidentiality in a deep way, not fix, save, correct or advise anyone (truly a hard guideline for those of us in the helping professions to follow!), attend to your own inner teacher as you participate, and trust moments of silence without succumbing to the urge to fill them with words. By following these touchstones, you set aside many of the mental distractions and issues I've described that interfere with being aware of your inner wisdom, particularly the group pressures to meet other people's expectations and deal with their opinions and judgments.

By creating and being part of this safe "intentional community," as Parker would describe it, you are better able to stay open to the positive but often subtle input you receive from your inner wisdom as you contemplate a question or issue in your personal life or work. Exploring that question or issue often involves taking a deeper inner dive by using what Parker calls "third things" – poems, stories, art, photographs, objects from nature, and natural processes such as the transition of the seasons – that act as metaphors for your inner process and help you engage more deeply with it. Circles of Trust also use practices such as journaling, periods of silence and reflection, and asking "open and honest questions" that encourage you to look within yourself for guidance from your inner teacher.

But that's not the whole story. Within Circles of Trust, Parker incorporates another Quaker practice, the Clearness Committee. This is a small group that supports an individual's discernment around a specific issue or question that's hard for them to get clarity about on their own. A Clearness Committee meets for about two hours at the request of a "focus person" to help that person become aware of the "inner light" (as Quakers would call it) that provides wisdom and direction. As he does in Circles of Trust, Parker takes a step away from the explicit spiritual language used by Quakers and writes about Clearness Committees helping the focus person become aware of their "inner teacher" or true self. From my perspective, this language is a perfectly fine middle ground to meet people who don't have a spiritual perspective on this process without putting off the people who do.

Building on the Circle of Trust touchstones, guidelines specific to a Clearness Committee are then added. A quiet, contemplative environment is created before and during a Clearness Committee by eliminating casual conversation and keeping silence before the committee begins its work. Members are also asked to limit their usual social interactions so they don't interfere with the focus person's inner experience. For instance, eye contact between the focus person and the committee members is discouraged, and committee members are advised to avoid subtle body language – head shakes or nods, or leaning in or out of the group, for example – that communicates your agreement or disagreement, approval or disapproval. To minimize this even further, the focus person is advised to either close their eyes for the entire time or to stay focused on a candle or centerpiece in the middle of the group.

After the Clearness Committee begins, the active work of the committee members consists of doing just one thing: asking the focus person open and honest questions. These are questions that are open-ended, without a simple yes-or-no answer, that are intended to encourage inner reflection. They are honest because they don't have a personal agenda or imply a right answer that puts subtle or not-so-subtle pressure on the focus person. For instance, the question "Have you thought about seeing a therapist for your problem?" or "Have you read chapter five of so-and-so's latest book?" are not open and honest questions. The questioner clearly has an idea of the best way forward and wants the focus person to "get it." However, questions like, "What are some other times in your life when you've had a similar experience?" or "What does this situation remind you of?" offer the focus person a chance to explore their question more deeply within themselves. Open and honest questions maintain safe space while creating fertile ground for the focus person's wise inner self to explore a new perspective.

In preparing people for a Clearness Committee, I've discovered that it's important to make sure the members buy into its assumptions and processes. During one committee I facilitated, an inexperienced member seriously disrupted the process by repeatedly making encouraging and supportive statements to the focus person. Afterwards, he told me that the Clearness Committee process felt unnatural to him, even to the extent that he felt he was violating his own principles and betraying the years of supportive counseling he had done with troubled military veterans facing difficulties. He felt that it was essential for him to express his genuine caring and support for the focus person in the earnest, concerned and engaged way he usually did.

I explained to him that what a Clearness Committee does is different from the normal practice of offering positive support, encouragement and approval, which as a psychotherapist I'd also had considerable experience with. In this unique process, you're offering something unusual – the opportunity to open to insight – that the focus person has specifically asked for. Even if it feels awkward, in order to create the possibility for deep insight that you've promised, you need to set aside your agenda of making that person feel encouraged, supported and even cared for in the ordinary way you might do that. As Parker describes it:

> *We are to hold the soul of the focus person as if we were holding a small bird in the palms of our two hands. As we do so, we are likely to experience three temptations, and we must resist all of them: to take this creature apart and find out what makes it tick…to let our attention flag, mind wander, or no longer hold the focus person at the center of our awareness…or to let our cupped hands make a subtle but persistent upward motion, encouraging the bird to fly.*

By taking such exquisite care in defining our intentions and practices, Circles of Trust or Clearness Committees can often accomplish what no other group process in my experience can do: make it possible for someone struggling with a personal issue or question to receive genuine insight about it. This is truly worth the effort of setting aside our conventional social interactions and doing things differently.

A personal experience

The most remarkable experience I've had as the focus person of a Clearness Committee was during a retreat on Bainbridge Island near Seattle. This beautiful and peaceful retreat center is set in a thick forest with large and small log cabins and meeting spaces connected by a network of trails. It is exactly the sort of environment to encourage people to set aside their usual life concerns and connect with their inner awareness. My six-person committee met in a small log cabin with a fireplace, and as we settled into the rough handmade chairs with the fire burning comfortably and a candle on a table between us, I felt relaxed yet a little uneasy about exploring an issue that troubled me.

I had long been concerned about how much to get involved with issues around diversity, racism and justice, which I care about deeply. I also have considerable experience with my personal limitations at addressing topics that evoke a lot of emotion. Even with all I know and practice to maintain a sense of balance and inner peace, I can get overwhelmed when I get too involved in issues that I feel passionate or conflicted about. So the question I brought to the Clearness Committee was: What is the best role for me to take around social justice and diversity issues? Should I leave them to others, or risk plunging in over my head?

The committee members asked a number of open and honest questions, and I felt that the first half-hour or so was very helpful. Then, out of the blue, one of the committee members asked an open and honest question that seemed completely irrelevant and had nothing to do with what had come before. "What hobbies do you have?" he asked.

I was thrown off balance, and considered passing on the question, which is something a focus person can do since they are in charge of their own process. Then, with a bit of resigned impatience and wanting to get on with it, I briefly described my interest in amateur astronomy and soccer, inwardly hoping that we'd get back to what seemed like a more relevant line of questions. Which we did, for a few minutes.

Then someone on the committee asked me, "If being involved in race and diversity issues was like being on a soccer team, what position would you be playing?"

At that moment, I felt an inward opening, a comfortable *ahh...*

of understanding that was clear and right. It was the perfect open and honest question, and my inner wisdom instantly knew how to respond.

I'd be a creative midfielder, I said. I'd link the defense and the offense. I wouldn't score a lot of goals myself, but I'd create opportunities for other people to score. I can see myself creating opportunities and offering ideas for others to engage with justice and diversity issues, and occasionally doing something directly myself when the situation calls for it.

This was the perfect insight I needed, and an explicit answer to the question I'd brought to the committee.

I don't remember exactly how the Clearness Committee continued to the end. But I do recall that a couple of minutes after the insight came to me, one of the committee members leaned forward and said, "Shhh... be very quiet, and look out the window." I turned my head to the right, and about a dozen feet outside the window were three deer, looking in at us calmly and with curiosity. They knew something special had happened, and so did we.

A few months later, I volunteered to be a facilitator for *Celebrate Diversity,* an organization in my community that works with groups and organizations in northeast Wisconsin to promote understanding and acceptance of people who are seen as "other" and often treated unjustly. As a facilitator, the role I play is that of "creative midfielder," creating safe space and helping others find their own way into these difficult and potentially emotional issues. The insight I received enables me to work for a cause I care about without being overwhelmed by it.

Being ourselves

I'm sure that the specific insight I gained in this experience wasn't the only one possible. Talking about my interest in soccer naturally led to the idea of being a "creative midfielder," but a different process might have resulted in a similarly useful insight, even if it didn't come forward in exactly those words. For instance, taking on the role of "creative midfielder" is not much different than acting as a "catalyst" or being an "actively engaged resource person." The bottom line is that asking for my deepest truth in the Clearness Committee process led me to a personally meaningful realization.

Everyone has a unique experience of their inner wisdom. Whatever that experience may be, how you think of it and the relationship you create with it is at the heart of what you experience as being human. How your life unfolds and your sense of who you are will be profoundly different whether you are actively involved with your inner wisdom every day, ask for it only when you're facing a particular problem or issue, or ignore it completely. Clearly, your inner wisdom is essential to speaking your true thoughts and feelings, connecting deeply in your closest relationships, discerning your life's purpose, being personally fulfilled, and experiencing your genuine humanity.

It's a wonderful opportunity – the opportunity of a lifetime – to embrace a relationship with your inner wisdom that reflects the deepest truth you know about who you are and what your life is about. Maybe you'll relate to it as the presence of God, your true self, the inner light, an angel or spirit guide, or as simply a different way of thinking. Whatever you believe your inner wisdom is and what you think your relationship with it should be, you have ample reason to welcome and be grateful for it. Accepting its reality and actively asking for it will make your life fertile ground where the deepest truth you know can come alive.

This is a poem I wrote to a psychotherapy client after we had finished our work together. It's about asking for the truth of the moment that leads you into the larger truth of your life.

A T'AI CHI FOR YOU

*open and round
new moon's pale edge
mind curves   hand follows*

Your mind moves   your life follows.
My hope and prayer:
your mind moves towards happiness
your life towards joy

It is all about you and your bravery
the truth and your willingness to speak truth
and look at yourself
fearlessly   with compassion

It has been my joy to see you whole
to see the whole person alive
inside you   ahead of you
beyond your daily pain

Trust this: there is goodness to come
great passion and love
your life and art
creating you   recreating you

Walk your path   do the work
It is not always hard
sometimes what is simple
is just right

Your heart knows the way

Chapter 5

Understanding Inner Wisdom

Do not understand me too quickly.

– André Gide

For many years, on the wall of my psychotherapy office I displayed the advice from novelist André Gide to his literary critics that they not understand him "too quickly." He was asking, of course, that they not limit themselves to first impressions and a superficial understanding of his writing. I explained to new psychotherapy clients that this was largely a reminder to me not to jump to conclusions about them and to take time to understand them more completely. If they wanted to take his advice and not understand me too quickly either, that would be fine, too.

It is hard advice to follow, though. When you look at other people or at the world, you often limit yourself to your preconceived or simplistic ideas about what you see. That's all too often how you look at and understand yourself, as well. For all of us, our blindness is seldom greater than when we look in the mirror. We're wise to be humble about the understanding we have of ourselves and what we're doing in the world.

Similarly, it's wise to hold your understanding of inner wisdom lightly and let it evolve as you have more experience with it. It's all too human to label or categorize your initial experiences of it "too quickly," depending on what you believe about yourself and others, and about how the world works. But by doing so, you may miss some of the mystery that is part of inner wisdom. It takes time to begin to grasp the deep nature of who you are and your relationship with other living beings. You may also find it worthwhile to take a step back and think as clearly as you can about what this process is and what part it should play in your life.

For instance, you might ask: Is inner wisdom a good thing or a bad thing? Could it be God speaking – or perhaps the devil – and how would I know the difference? Or is it my own higher self or true self? The guidance of my ancestors? A spirit guide? A normal psychological process? An abnormal psychological process, such as a delusion or hallucination? A neuropsychological process that's activating part of my brain in an unusual way? Or does it point to something fundamental about who I am as a human being?

The ideas – and apprehensions – you may have about your inner wisdom inevitably reflect your cultural, spiritual, and intellectual theories and beliefs. During my own life journey, I have grown to think of myself as a spiritual being deeply embedded in a world of light, love, and mystery, and involved in a personal process of growth and realization much larger and more remarkable than I can rationally understand. At the same time, I also think of myself as a psychologist and scientist who respects natural laws and processes and has a great curiosity and sense of humility about the way our biology and life experiences guide and shape us, even while I believe that our physical self and personal history are far from the whole story. Both perspectives immerse me in questions about my inner wisdom that I find interesting and personally important.

Here's a short list of some of the questions that have intrigued and challenged me about inner wisdom. My musings are certainly not comprehensive, but they do reflect my own personal journey as I learn and grow.

1. As a psychologist, how do I see inner wisdom?
2. How do I see inner wisdom as a spiritual person?
3. Why does inner wisdom exist?
4. Is inner wisdom a good thing or a bad thing?
5. How can I know that an insight is truly from my inner wisdom?
6. Is there something I need to believe about inner wisdom for it to show up?

1. As a psychologist, how do I see inner wisdom?

Psychologists try to understand how human beings think, feel and act in the world, and those of us involved with clinical psychology or positive psychology are very much interested in what humans can do to live happier and better lives. So the process of becoming aware of the deepest truth you know, and the challenge of living it, is squarely in the middle of the psychological experiences of interest to me.

From my own professional perspective and personal experience, inner wisdom is not a mental health problem. The insights as I've described and experienced them are not delusional beliefs, hallucinatory processes from a disordered brain, or signs of a thought disorder such as schizophrenia. They do not reflect "an underlying psychobiological dysfunction" that creates "clinically significant distress (e.g., a painful symptom) or disability (i.e., impairment in one or more important areas of functioning)," as the fifth edition of the *Diagnostic and Statistical Manual of Mental Disorders (DSM-5)* defines psychopathology. In my experience, inner wisdom may challenge social constraints and personal limitations, but it does so in a way that is aligned with personal growth and healing. It offers deep truths about your life, and following them – or ignoring them – can have a profound effect on your personal happiness and fulfillment.

Partly because of my difficult personal life as I was growing up, what most intrigues me about taking a psychological perspective on inner wisdom is the personal and social challenge of letting our deep truth come forward. I often feel – and I know others feel as well – tension between the pressure to go along with the wishes of others, and the subtle but insistent desire to find a way of understanding and acting that is genuine and intrinsic to me. Finding the balance between these two parts of myself, and learning how to trust inner wisdom and have the courage to act on it, has been a defining issue in my life.

The brokenness of my early years also made me aware of the deep need that I and others have to become whole. Becoming a psychologist was a natural part of that path: my own growth required me to learn to see other people as whole, and to help them live the whole truth of their lives. That whole truth embraces inner wisdom, and it also embraces the process of healing. The Old English word *haelan* means "to heal" or "to make whole." Healing and becoming whole is mysterious, because it goes well beyond the limited medical definition of "curing," which is usually thought of as making a problem go away and reestablishing the status quo. A deeper healing or making whole may mean discovering what is missing and restoring it, but it can also result in personal growth, a deeper sense of self and relationship with others, and a renewal of spiritual awareness. My own healing and growth have led to many new realizations about who I am and what I need to be and do in the world.

In my professional role as a psychologist, helping others heal and become whole has taught me other important lessons as well. One of these is humility. I don't always understand everything going on with my clients, can't always predict what they will do, and certainly can't control the outcome of therapy, solve their problems and make them happier. What I can do, I've learned, is keep showing up humbly and compassionately with the best of myself that I'm able to bring forth in the moment. Similarly, when I commit to being open to my own inner wisdom's insights, I know that what I discover will not be predictable, controllable, and understandable in a conventional sense. My human limitations as a healer and a psychologist have helped me discern and accept whatever may come from my inner wisdom.

I've also learned the value of trusting the process. I may not have control over the outcome of my healing and counseling work, but something good is happening – and although I may not fully understand how, my way of being and doing is part of that. I trust that something good will come of the process we're engaged in because of the positive caring intention I hold for the person in front of me, the deep respect and warm regard I have for that person, and the genuine (if limited) relationship I am committed to build with them. Similarly in my own life, because of the remarkable insights I've received from my inner wisdom over the years I have learned to accept and trust the process of asking for guidance and acting on it, even if I don't specifically know where it will lead me.

My work has also helped me become more committed and courageous. When I started out doing psychotherapy as a brand-new graduate student, I was reluctant to hear about painful events in other people's lives because they evoked my own unhealed pain. In fact, listening to my clients' painful stories was initially so difficult for me that my attention would involuntarily wander and I'd often miss key things they told me. At first, I was embarrassed by this, but then alarmed: if I couldn't change this dissociative response and hear what my clients were telling me, I couldn't do psychotherapy and would have to drop out of my graduate program. It took nearly a year of hard work on myself to learn to focus my attention and really hear what other people said about their lives, however uncomfortable it was for me. Again, I found that I needed to bring a similar commitment to becoming aware of my inner wisdom, accepting it as it is and having the courage to act on it.

I've learned more from being a healer and psychotherapist that supports living the deepest truth I know, but those are some of the things that have mattered most to me. Looking back, it's not surprising that the deep impulse I felt to become a psychologist was guided by my inner wisdom. I have grown profoundly by taking on the challenges and accepting the gifts of this work.

2. How do I see inner wisdom as a spiritual person?

Long before I became a psychologist, I was a spiritual person. Growing up in a Lutheran family, by the time I was a teenager I found myself in considerable conflict with what I heard and was told to believe in church. Still, I went through the motions of doing what others expected me to do, though I sometimes stood silent when I didn't believe in the words I was supposed to say. Finally, just a few weeks after I completed the Lutheran process of confirmation in the faith when I was sixteen, I stopped going to church – or more accurately, I started searching for something that wasn't just about saying what I was told to say and that better represented my own experiential spirituality. Where could I find wisdom that rang true to me personally in a deep way?

Since that time, I've had meaningful spiritual experiences with the Unitarian-Universalist Fellowship, t'ai chi, meditation groups, new age churches, energy healing, a Course in Miracles, a Southern Baptist congregation, the Church of Spiritual Healing, several Unity Churches, the United Church of Christ, and most recently, the Religious Society of Friends (also known as Quakers). I've learned from these varied experiences that wisdom comes in many forms and from many sources, and that it is more important to test that wisdom against my own sense of its rightness and relevance for my life than it is to look outside myself for sources of validation. Ultimately, I've decided that it is my life and my responsibility to find a way forward spiritually that feels true to me and suits me best.

Most people seeking to understand and cultivate the deepest truth they know do so from a spiritual perspective. Listening for the "still, small voice" of God, or the "inward teacher" as Quakers traditionally called it, has long been part of religions around the world and throughout time. I am particularly drawn to the Quaker perspective on this. While acknowledging that sacred texts such as the Bible, the Torah, the Koran, the Vedas and Upanishads, the Tripitaka and Sutras, the Tao Te Ching, and many other texts may be spiritually inspired and offer wisdom for living, Quakers believe that the people who wrote those texts were inspired in the same way that any of us can be spiritually inspired today. The central belief at the heart of Quakerism is that "there is that of God in each of us." Friends make it a priority to attend to their own inner guidance and to discern carefully what is and what is not of God, both in Quaker meetings for worship and in daily life.

So if there is something of God in everyone, what is God? And what is our relationship with God, if God is the source of inner wisdom? There are probably as many answers to these questions as there are people reading this, and my own ideas about them have evolved over the years as well. I've come to think of God as a conscious, loving presence that generally moves me (and sometimes specifically guides me) toward love, fulfillment, healing, and personal and spiritual growth. In my best and most aware moments, this is the living experience of loving and being loved, connecting and being connected, in the deepest way I've ever known. As the Sufi poet Rumi says, it is the ecstasy of dancing with the Beloved. In my more mundane daily life, it is the grace of never feeling lonely, even when I'm alone.

Patricia Loring, a Friend who's written extensively about Quaker practice, has a similar perspective. She notes that modern Friends often consider God as a "dynamism" moving within each person rather than an entity "standing outside and giving orders, pulling strings or whispering instructions in order to stage-manage history." When you choose to be aware of and follow your inner wisdom, you are co-creative with the inner dynamism of God. You're collaboratively creating your world by building an active and engaged relationship with the source of your inner wisdom. As Loring puts it, to look for and follow inner wisdom is to "respond in faithfulness to the promptings of Love and Truth in our hearts."

As I look back at my spiritual journey, I realize that in following "the promptings of Love and Truth" in my heart, my goal was not only to find a deep truth to guide my personal life but to find ways to be of service to the world. That focus on meaningful service started early and grew stronger when I learned how to do energy healing and worked with people with AIDS, and then continued to volunteer with hospice patients, the homeless, and others. It played a significant role in my becoming a clinical health psychologist, and then led me to transform my work yet again to help others attain insight and clarity about their lives. At present, I find the Quaker religion to be a comfortable home for my spirituality in large part because Quakers are steeped in spiritual service aligned with inner wisdom. The Quaker practice of silent worship is a conscious path toward opening to the guidance of spirit, integrating it into daily life and meeting the needs of others.

Given my varied spiritual background, it also feels natural to me to use language that is open and inclusive to describe this process. It's obvious by now that I usually describe the loving presence of God manifesting itself as *inner wisdom*. Because this phrase is grounded in the experience of discerning guidance from within, it is usually understood and accepted by people from many spiritual traditions and by non-spiritual people as well.

But I'm not exclusively committed to that phrase, even though I've used it throughout this book. Other descriptions of the source of our inner wisdom that I like include the Quaker characterizations of the "inner teacher" or "inner light," the phrase "true self" adopted by Trappist monk Thomas Merton and Franciscan friar Richard Rohr, the 12-step program language of "higher power" or "guidance," and even the Biblical "still, small voice." As a more general term for what is essential about humans, I particularly like the word "soul," which reflects something deeply personal about us that is beyond our physical and psychological self. Thinking of inner wisdom as an active and conscious connection with our soul gracefully embraces both its spiritual and personal aspects.

3. Why does inner wisdom exist?

This is certainly an intriguing question. Does inner wisdom's ability to help resolve personal problems and questions have biological survival value, and is it therefore a trait that evolved in human beings? If you take a more spiritual view, does its presence mean that people were created to have a close and personal relationship with God? Or perhaps describing inner wisdom as having some simple purpose is not really the point. Could it better to think of it as simply part of the deep, inexplicable nature of human beings, as you might think of your DNA, multicellular structure, and human consciousness?

All of these views have validity in their own context, and they all point to the idea that inner wisdom is a deep and integral part of our nature. Here's psychologist Carl Rogers' take on that idea. He saw the drive behind inner wisdom as something more fundamental than a specific adaptive characteristic that helped humans survive an evolutionary competition. Rogers proposed that all organisms (meaning humans and other living beings) have a basic "actualizing tendency" that moves them toward more complex and complete development – which is not so different than the loving, healing, growing and unifying force that I personally think of as the source of inner wisdom. He thought of this actualizing tendency as "the very nature of the process we call life."

To illustrate this, Rogers used an example from his childhood: he noticed that potatoes stored in the basement would futilely attempt to grow shoots to get sunlight and extend roots in search of water and nourishment. Their physical growth and movement toward the resources they needed was an example of all the things we do to live and grow. Most importantly, he saw this central activating principle and living force as part of our psychology and personhood. It energizes us to heal from traumatic and painful hurts and moves us to try to live whole and happy lives.

Based on his many interactions with patients as well as his own and others' observations, Rogers theorized that this striving toward healing and wholeness is part of our essential nature as living beings. That certainly makes sense to me. In my own experience as a therapist, I have often seen this striving in people I've counseled who have worked through personal problems and gained new insight about their life. Whether you're healing from terrible trauma or simply finding a way to answer a question or resolve an issue, your inner wisdom manifests a "potent constructive tendency," as Rogers called it, to maintain, enhance and fulfill your life.

From a more explicitly spiritual perspective, some believe that our inner wisdom exists because a loving God wants to be in relationship with us. My own experience with an inner loving presence tells me that this relationship is probably not something unchanging and blissful, or something that exists to reward good behavior. In my life, loving and being loved hasn't been static or passive. Rather, it's brought me learning, change and personal growth. It's also not conditional on my believing and doing the right things. Loving and being loved is what makes learning and change possible.

UNDERSTANDING INNER WISDOM

As I experience it, inner wisdom is a purposeful tool that guides my growth and change, and it arises naturally out of my relationship with the active loving presence of God. Opening myself to that inner presence of love and truth helps me grow as a person, and I am always learning how to deeply trust it and live courageously according to its guidance. So for me, from a spiritual perspective, the purpose of my inner wisdom is to energize my spiritual and personal growth and bring love and truth into the center of my relationships and activities.

Inner wisdom also exists for a collective and social purpose. As I've learned, there are ways we can engage with others that actively support and serve their deep truth and who they really are. In our conflicted world, this is increasingly important. Parker Palmer notes that there are many forces in our increasingly technological society that pressure us to deny or diminish our humanity. There's the anonymous hostility and conflict that occur on the Internet, the pressures and demands of social media, the businesses that manipulate us to give them our attention and money, the politicians that arouse our anger and fear to get our support, and so on. In the face of these dehumanizing social forces, inner wisdom has another reason to exist: it enables us to acknowledge and care for the humanity of others. It is a place to stand against the cultural waves that attempt to make all of us less than we are. As Parker says,

> *For "it" (our soul) is the objective, ontological reality of selfhood that keeps us from reducing ourselves, or each other, to biological mechanisms, psychological projections, sociological constructs, or raw material to be manufactured into whatever society needs – diminishments of our humanity that constantly threaten the quality of our lives.*

In other words, the deepest truth you know is important not just to your own life, but to the deepest appreciation you can have of others and your life with them.

4. Is inner wisdom a good thing or a bad thing?

I suspect that if you've read this far, you probably think inner wisdom is a good thing – and I agree. However, although I've been describing our inner wisdom in positive ways, I believe there are reasons to be thoughtful about this question. In one sense, whether inner wisdom is a good or bad thing is (in a favorite phrase of one of my graduate school advisors) an "empirical question" that can be answered from your own experience. If your inner wisdom leads you toward positive experiences, then you could reasonably consider the process that got you there to be a good one. As rationally inexplicable as it was for me to move to Kansas City, I'm certainly glad I did because it had a good outcome for me.

On the other hand, what is a good outcome? Is it getting what you logically think you want and simply affirming what you've already figured out is best? Your inner wisdom often doesn't do that, and may lead you down a different path than your rational or social-approval-seeking mind might want. Or is it a good outcome when your inner wisdom sometimes surprises you, challenges you, and even distresses you by offering you a truth that is uncomfortable for you to hear or see? To be open to this second possibility, you need to hold the idea of "good" rather broadly and selflessly. In my experience, the good outcomes that result from following your inner wisdom usually do one of two things: they either fulfill and affirm you in some positive way or they present you with a challenge that leads to your personal or spiritual growth.

For many people, though, a good outcome may be more about trusting the process than evaluating the results. They might not trust a process that's outside their conscious, rational control, that isn't part of their belief system, or that's simply different than the usual way they deal with questions and issues. So if a person believes that they can only trust a rational cost-benefit analysis of the material facts relevant to their life choices (for example, determining what job will pay the most), they may dismiss insight coming from their inner wisdom as irrelevant "noise" or even as delusional self-deception. Similarly, if a person has spiritual beliefs that lead them to distrust experiences that are described with unfamiliar language and are not accepted and approved by their religious tradition (for instance, receiving an insight that didn't result from a specific prayer to Jesus, Krishna, or Allah), they may dismiss their inner wisdom as a negative or demonic influence.

Of course, inner wisdom is fully capable of operating within a specific religious, spiritual or intellectual belief system, and usually does. However, it is not necessary to hold a particular set of beliefs in order to experience it. Whatever your belief system may be, I encourage you to create a warmly inviting context for your inner wisdom. You can then decide based on your own experience whether the process is good for you.

5. How can I know that an insight is truly from my inner wisdom?

Suppose you get past your initial resistances and are willing to engage with your inner wisdom. Even then, you still face the challenge of discerning whether a particular insight is coming from an authentic place. It is essential to learn how to identify in yourself "the sound of the genuine," as writer and civil rights leader Howard Thurman put it. Early on for me, this was a relatively easy thing. My inner wisdom simply had such a sense of truth and reality about it that I had no problem distinguishing it from my ordinary thoughts. I was comfortable following it because it felt positive, even when it suggested such major changes as a move to another city.

It wasn't always so clear, though. As I opened to inner wisdom around other decisions, particularly those that were emotional and personal, I needed to discover my self-deceptions and personal pitfalls, distinguish them from my genuine inner wisdom, and learn to set them aside. As I discussed earlier, I especially needed to discern when my insight was simply a way of supporting my personal agenda, justifying "whatever I want," or following what other people wanted me to do. You, too, will need to discern whether your insight is your own deepest truth or simply reflects your own personal desires or someone else's beliefs and priorities. Making these distinctions takes time and patience. It requires you to develop self-awareness and personal maturity, both psychological and spiritual. It may also sometimes mean that you say "no" to opportunities that seem superficially attractive.

One key element of genuine discernment that I've often experienced is a simple one: Am I surprised by what my inner wisdom presents to me, at least a little, because it wasn't what I was expecting? It may be a new idea, which leads to a sense of revelation. Or sometimes perhaps it's more of a puzzled surprise: the insight that I needed to find a t'ai chi class in Kansas City was credible in part because it was completely unexpected and I didn't initially understand its purpose. Insight from your inner wisdom may not always come as a surprise, however. It may come as a deep knowing that resolves some of your tension around a question or issue. The resulting sense of resolution often affirms that you're on the right track and gives you confidence in taking your next step.

Discernment isn't always an individual process, however. As I mentioned earlier, Quakers come to the process of discernment from the perspective that there is "that of God in each of us" and "an inner light" guiding us, which provides a solid spiritual framework for accepting inner wisdom. However, in addition to developing the essential individual characteristics of self-awareness, trust, and spiritual maturity needed to discern God's guidance, Quakers recommend that at least sometimes you thoughtfully look to others who are spiritually mature as well. As a Quaker, Parker Palmer suggests that embedding yourself in a supportive, caring community with positive values in line with your own is essential to provide a context for your inner wisdom and help you better understand its message.

However, consulting with others about your inner wisdom's guidance isn't about asking for their approval or whether the insight you've received seems appropriate, practical, or worthwhile to them – at least, you shouldn't let it be! If you do consult with others regarding the guidance you've received, choose people who are experienced enough to help you understand it more deeply for yourself. Similar to the process you might experience in a Clearness Committee, your advisors might do that by deeply listening and asking open and honest questions.

The people who do this best are likely to be in touch with their own inner wisdom and to understand how important it is to create safe space for it and respect it. When I consult others about the guidance of my inner wisdom, the response is generally positive and affirming, and I often come away with a deeper understanding of my guidance or a different way to act on it. I'm confident in saying that while inner wisdom may be subtle, it's also strong, and it won't be blown away like a leaf in the wind when other people help you explore it in a respectful way.

6. Is there something I need to believe about inner wisdom for it to show up?

When I graduated from college and received the insights to create space in my life to write and then to move to Kansas City, I didn't have a spiritual perspective or a particular set of beliefs that validated my inner wisdom. However, unlike my ordinary rational process of solving problems or figuring things out that was full of uncertainty and alternative possibilities, my inner wisdom's guidance had a feeling of truth and reality that simply felt right to act on.

Based on that, it was clear to me for a long time that inner wisdom was simply part of being human. I didn't think about it much – I simply acted on it, and learned in doing so that I could trust it to lead me into good experiences. I didn't believe anything in particular about what it was or where it came from. Even today, I'd say that what you believe about inner wisdom is not the most important thing. The experience of inner wisdom and guidance is part of the lives of people from many different cultures and widely differing beliefs, and can be understood from a broad range of scientific, philosophical, psychological and spiritual perspectives. It certainly doesn't require a particular spiritual belief or membership in a specific religion, and you don't need a training program or a special initiation in order to experience it.

That said, as I've grown spiritually and considered more deeply the nature of my experience of inner wisdom and its role in my life, my understanding of it has grown. I've come to believe that inner wisdom arises out of my relationship with a conscious loving spiritual presence that is both part of and beyond who I am. When I open to that spiritual presence, inner wisdom arises in a way that is positive, growth-enhancing, and transformational. It links who I am with the underlying reality of the world in ways that current scientific theories and my limited ego can't explain. As a result, I now ask for inner wisdom with more reverence and respect than I did earlier in my life. I also take greater care to create positive intentions and circumstances that facilitate the process. Asking for guidance connects me with a profound part of myself and the universe, and deserves to be approached with a bit of awe.

If you're just beginning the exploration of your inner wisdom, I encourage you to treat it as a personal process that you take seriously, and not as an intellectual game or experiment to "see if it works." To have a genuine experience of inner wisdom, you need to be vulnerable and humble enough to ask sincerely for the deepest truth you know about a personal question or issue, and then be open to a possibly surprising response that may come to you in an unexpected way. If you sincerely seek your deepest truth about something important to you, my own experience and that of many others is that you can receive insight that is wise and good. Whatever your belief system or cultural tradition may be, you're welcome to verify this for yourself – and I hope you will.

I wrote this in Kansas City when I worked for New Letters Magazine to honor the life and work of the magazine's celebrated calligrapher. It is about the deep power and wisdom behind the surface of what we know and do. The final three lines are one of Lloyd's own haiku.

LLOYD REYNOLDS, CALLIGRAPHER
in memoriam

It's not
so much
what exists.

Pen strokes
are the easy
answers.

In between
is the pause
the white space

the inhalation
that is everything
we mean

beyond words
the force
behind words –

Blizzard!
it's white
between the snowflakes

Chapter 6

Mission and Purpose

Your purpose in life is to find your purpose, and give your whole heart and soul to it.

– Gautama Buddha

One of the most surprising pieces of guidance I've received came after I moved to Atlanta. I had thought that I would be teaching people how to bring spiritual insights into their daily lives. Instead, I was inwardly led to become a corporate writer in the business community.

I didn't see this coming at all, and my inner wisdom's direction was clearly a surprise – partly because I had no experience or qualifications to do that work. It took me many months of knocking on doors (and unsuccessfully trying to make the case that having been on the radio somehow meant I could write corporate speeches and marketing materials) before I got my first job, which was with a successful business writer who had more work than he could do himself and was willing to take a risk on me. After a year of working for him, which allowed me to develop an impressive portfolio of work, he moved out of town and I set up my own freelance corporate writing business. The personal gift in it was that I got to discover what it was like to support myself doing something I loved, writing. In addition, it enabled me to move beyond my self-focused life as a poet and serve others who wanted to communicate clearly about things that were important to them. As part of the business world (completely new territory for me), I also learned more about people who were committed to that way of thinking and doing things.

After six years as corporate writer in Atlanta, though, it became clear that it was again time to move on. The business world had been interesting and I'd been financially successful in it. But as I told people at the time, "My soul has nothing else to say about Diet Coke®." So I committed myself to what I believed was a thoughtful, deliberate process of personal exploration to determine my next step.

I again had a strong urge to move to a new city to help myself start with a clean slate. This time, Chicago was calling to me. I had enough money in the bank to survive for about eight months without working, if I was careful. So I got a cheap North Side apartment on Lake Michigan to be close to water, which I love. Just for fun, I also signed up for painting and drawing classes at the Chicago Art Institute. To discover what was next for me, I took vocational aptitude and interest tests, participated in personal growth workshops, read numerous books on career development, and spent a great deal of time thinking about what had been important in my life.

After several months of outer assessment and inner searching, my new path in life became clear. With considerable excitement and a sense that I was going to pursue work that was close to my heart and would do some good in the world, I decided to start a career as a volunteer coordinator in a hospital or similar service organization, and perhaps teach a high school class on being a community volunteer. I was delighted to discover that some private schools actually hired people to teach about volunteering, and there were plenty of hospitals in the area. I was happy and excited about my new direction, and ready to go.

My excitement lasted three days. Then it hit me that being a volunteer coordinator and teaching about volunteering asked nothing of me that I couldn't already do and, for the most part, that I hadn't already done. Using the corporate lingo I'd been immersed in for the previous six years, it was a way of "repackaging" who I already was, but it wasn't about growing into who I could become. I certainly hadn't found a purpose I could "give my whole heart and soul to," as the Buddha said. More than a little disappointed and frustrated that all my self-exploration had led to such a superficial conclusion about my future, I gave up the search. No more vocational questionnaires, thank you. Still, I hoped that what I needed to do next would somehow become clear.

One morning a few weeks later, I was in downtown Chicago returning a book for a friend to the Northwestern University Medical School library, and something led me to ask permission to wander through the library for a while. As I walked past the books, a title grabbed my attention and almost seemed to jump off the shelf: *Medicine as a Human Experience*, by David Reiser and David Rosen. The authors were physicians at the University of Rochester School of Medicine and Dentistry in New York. Standing there in the library, I read a few pages and was hooked. Written for medical students and residents, the book is about person-centered relationships between doctors and patients, communication issues in the medical world, and humane ways of approaching professional activities. I did the best sales job of my life and persuaded the librarian to let me check it out.

After I finished reading that book, I felt a deep sense of excitement and calling. I knew profoundly that I had something to contribute to the conversation about how doctors and patients communicate. I even had experience I could draw on. I was a writer, after all, and hadn't I worked with business professionals and interviewed dozens of people on radio? But I needed to find a way into the conversation. I didn't want to become an MD and learn how to apply thousands of facts to treating medical diseases. What seemed right was to become a health psychologist, which would let me work with medical patients around personal issues related to their illnesses. The master's degree I'd received would get me into a graduate program, and a Ph.D. in psychology would give me the credential and experience I'd need to help physicians learn to communicate in more patient-centered ways.

What a revelation! For the first time in my life, I felt a strong sense of mission and purpose. This work was genuinely important to others, and it felt both humbling and wonderful to feel called to it. It was also a huge commitment. I was thirty-five, and for the next six years I would be in graduate school and doing clinical training. But since I was going to be doing *something* when I turned forty-one, why shouldn't it be work I loved that gave me a sense of purpose? I felt deep satisfaction in knowing that once again, my life was unfolding in exactly the way it needed it to.

A walk on the beach

A month or so after I decided to become a psychologist, however, I realized that I was committing myself to do something I'd never done before: listen to people talk all day long. As a writer, I'd often had long periods of time alone and I usually enjoyed solitude. So before I signed up for six years of training to spend the rest of my career with people telling me about personal things that concerned them, I wanted to find out what it was like to do psychotherapy. Maybe I could sit in on a psychotherapy group or witness some one-on-one sessions. I wanted to confirm for myself that this was something I could enjoy. But how could I make that happen?

A few days later, I was walking down my street and a neighbor I'd become friends with came out on her porch with another person. She beckoned me over. "This is my friend Sharon," she said. "She's a psychotherapist and wants to write a book about her work. I told her you were a writer and might be willing to talk with her about how she could that."

I suggested we take a walk on the beach near my apartment, which was just half a block away. As we walked, Sharon described her work, the psychotherapy clinic she led, and the sort of book she wanted to write. I told her I'd been a writer and had a writing business in Atlanta, and I made some suggestions for how she might organize her book and get herself into a regular writing routine. Then I told her that I'd recently decided to become a psychologist and work with medical patients and professionals. But I didn't have any experience doing psychotherapy, and I felt I needed to make sure the work suited me before I made such a big commitment. We went up to my apartment and I showed her some of the books I'd been reading about personal and spiritual growth, many of which turned out to be books she owned, too.

"I need someone to do part-time administrative work in my clinic a few days a week," she said. "Why don't you come do that for me, and you can sit in on some of the therapy groups I lead. After you see what we're doing, maybe you can even co-lead them."

It was just what I'd inwardly asked for, and it showed up in the most unexpected way I could have imagined. I worked in her clinic for the next nine months until I went off to graduate school. I learned what it took to run the business end of a psychotherapy clinic, and I found it quite interesting (though challenging) to co-lead a therapy group. I also made just enough money at the job to keep going until I started school.

This remarkable experience affirmed for me that my inner wisdom's guidance toward a career in psychology was being supported in ways I couldn't and still can't explain. What is clear to me, though, is that trusting and committing myself to the deepest truth I knew helped me find the way forward that was right for me. It doesn't always happen in such an extraordinary way, but following your deepest truth can bring you together with resources both inside yourself and out in the world that are beyond what you already know.

Shifting gears

It wasn't until I looked back at what I went through to start down the path of becoming a psychologist that I realized how powerfully and subtly my inner wisdom had been working with me. Far from being pointless, all the "right" things I did to change careers (take aptitude tests, read career development books, participate in personal growth workshops) were necessary at the time to shake me loose from my limited sense of myself. I could not have immediately jumped from being a corporate writer to concluding that I needed to get a Ph.D. and work with medical patients and physicians. As a first step in my learning, inner wisdom led me into those mundane, real-world processes so that I could discover more about who I was at that time.

The second step in the process was one of the most extraordinary learning experiences of my life. When I felt guided toward pursuing a career as a hospital volunteer coordinator, it was not because that was the work I was meant to do, but so I could clearly discern that this was *not* my new career! My inner wisdom painted me into a corner that was too small – and when I realized after three days that it was too small, it opened a door to let me find my way out. That deep part of me was perfectly aware of the unconscious limits holding me back, and knew exactly what I needed to do to release them and find my way forward.

Now that I knew what was next, I applied to twenty graduate school programs in clinical psychology. Even with my master's degree, I was accepted by just two of them. Fortunately, one was my top choice, the University of Rochester, where Drs. Reiser and Rosen had worked when they wrote their book. My interest in medical communication led me to kindred spirits at the University of Rochester medical school, and Dr. Tony Suchman generously invited me to be part of a two-year primary care medical fellowship that taught patient-centered medical interviewing, qualitative and quantitative research methods, the biopsychosocial model of medicine, and how to teach physicians and other medical staff. The fellowship ran simultaneously with the two most difficult years of my academic training in clinical psychology, and those years turned out to be the most intellectually challenging of my life. Still, that fellowship was one of the best gifts I'd ever received, and my whole heart and mind were engaged with learning new ideas and skills.

I was also growing in ways I hadn't anticipated. My sense of mission to help physicians communicate more effectively with their patients, I discovered, was also a prompt from my own inner wisdom to become kinder and more compassionate. Just as I had needed to move from my inwardly centered life as a poet to engage with others in the business world, I now needed to grow so I could be of service to people in a deeper and more personal way.

In the eyes of the world

On my journey toward finding a new career, I discovered that life doesn't always match up with the predictions of experts. For instance, vocational counselors often suggest that clients take a test that compares their own interests to those of a wide range of professionals. If your interests are similar to professionals in a particular area, the thinking goes, that might be a career to consider. When I moved to Chicago and took a career interest inventory, I discovered that my interests most closely coincided with those of librarians. That didn't surprise me, partly because I had several close friends who were librarians. At the same time, I knew that being a librarian wasn't for me. I like literature, but I don't like organizing books and keeping track of them, which someone could easily deduce by looking at the disorganized bookshelves scattered throughout my home and office.

Determining the right career by looking at work-related aptitudes runs into similar problems. Most job aptitude experts believe that being able to do something well is associated with enjoying it. Psychologists also know that being competent at something is enjoyable, but it's not the only consideration. During my self-exploration, a Johnson O'Connor career aptitude expert advised me that according to their assessment, I was far too slow at clerical speed and accuracy (basically, writing on paper with a pen) to enjoy being a writer. They call that skill "Graphoria," and I scored in the fourth percentile of all the writers in their massive database. Of course, I'd already had a successful career as a poet and corporate writer – and thankfully, I had started my corporate communications work when I could write more efficiently on a computer keyboard. The expert and I both smiled about that odd result.

In those months of exploration before I decided to become a psychologist, I was also advised that I needn't bother getting a doctoral degree – in anything. After giving me a personality assessment, a career expert told me that my personality wasn't really suited to "digging one deep hole, like a Ph.D. needs to do." To be a doctoral-level professional, she said, I needed to specialize, and my personality profile indicated that I was more of a generalist, interested in lots of things, and would be more satisfied "digging lots of shallow holes." Thankfully, I'd already had enough reasons to doubt experts about my career path to take her too seriously. But I did note that I probably would do better in a field where I could work with lots of different ideas, as I had done as a writer. Psychology gave me lots of options to dig deep or to focus more broadly, and it suited my personality just fine.

Fortunately, I was old enough and had enough experience of

the world to be able to keep what the experts told me in perspective. The opinions of people in a guidance role are sometimes much harder to deal with, though, particularly if you're a younger person. My wife was told when she was in high school that she "wasn't college material" because of her school performance, when in fact she had undiagnosed attention deficit disorder and dyslexia. When she finally entered college at twenty-four with a clear goal of becoming a physician, she received the appropriate medical treatment and testing accommodation. As a result, she's achieved a successful medical career that would have astounded her high school advisor.

Out of all the advice I received in Chicago about the career that was best for me, the most helpful message I heard was to choose something I liked and really wanted to do. But even that advice wasn't sufficient, because that's what I thought I'd done when I decided to become a hospital volunteer coordinator. I needed to take it to a deeper level than what I learned about myself from objective testing and career experts, and even from my own life experiences and preferences. I had to let my inner wisdom guide me into a career that truly reflected not only who I was, but the person I was ready to become.

There are compelling reasons to discover your own individual path, and what a difference it makes when you do. Emerson's famous essay from 1841, *Self-Reliance*, eloquently states the benefits of turning within to discover your unique perspective and talents.

> *Insist on yourself; never imitate. Your own gift you can present every moment with the cumulative force of a whole life's cultivation; but of the adopted talent of another, you have only an extemporaneous, half possession...Do that which is assigned to you, and you cannot hope too much or dare too much.*
>
> – Ralph Waldo Emerson

Personal issues and your deepest truth

As I've found in my own life, letting inner wisdom help you discover the vocation that's truly yours is one of the most rewarding experiences you can have. For me, it came out of a process of personal growth and learning over many years – I'm quite sure I wasn't capable of pursuing a career as a health psychologist when I first graduated from college, let alone immediately after my time as a corporate writer. However, as I grew personally and my life evolved in ways that allowed me to engage with that work, the path toward psychology opened for me in an energizing and positive way. Although some people might think it strange that a person in their late thirties would choose to go back to being a student, I'm grateful that I was not in any significant conflict with the people in my life or the cultural expectations around me.

But there was something else going on with that guidance as well: the personal growth I went through also arose out of some of my personal emotional issues. So what happens if, like me, you're being led toward a particular vocation or activity where you also have strong personal and perhaps unhealed feelings such as a sense of injustice, frustration, anger, or deep hurt?

I have to admit that my emotional reactivity has sometimes made it difficult for me to follow the deepest truth I know. Although my sense of calling to become a health psychologist was quite genuine, part of what drew me to work with communication and relationship issues in the medical field was my frustration with authority figures and my inner desire for physicians – or anyone with power – to listen better and be more caring and person-centered. Did that have any relationship to my own issues growing up with authoritative parents who didn't listen to me? Of course it did. For similar reasons, I had emotional difficulty when I got involved with social justice issues. I couldn't dive too deeply without feeling overwhelmed by frustration, anger and hopelessness, a clear sign that they triggered my own unhealed issues.

I am grateful to say that in both of these cases, and in others, the leadings into these activities became part of the healing I needed around my personal and family issues. In the course of my training as a health psychologist, and particularly in the medical fellowship where I learned patient-centered medical interviewing and how to acknowledge and accept medical patients as people as well as patients, I repeatedly observed senior physicians and psychologists treat patients with compassion for their medical condition, curiosity about their lives, and a genuine desire to help them live as well as they could with their problem. As I saw them treat others in the way I wished I'd been treated in my early life, it defused and healed much of the frustration and anger I'd been carrying with me and taught me to be more person-centered in my own work and personal life. Similarly, the experience I described of becoming a "creative midfielder" with *Celebrate Diversity* enabled me to place my personal anger at social injustice in a larger context, gave me constructive ways to act on it, and again, helped me heal some old hurts. In these situations and others, inner wisdom not only offered me a mission and purpose for my life, but led me to activities that allowed me to work through personal issues and grow in ways I needed to grow.

A calling to address social issues

The personal issues that motivate us aren't the whole story, however. There is work to be done to make the world a better place, and many of us feel called to do that work out of a desire to serve others or from compassion for the difficulties and suffering of others.

How does the process of following your deepest truth change if you feel called to challenge the ideas and values of the world – which inherently puts you in conflict with the society you live in? For example, what if the deepest truth you know is that you need to join our passionate, conflict-ridden social conversation and advocate for a cause you believe in, such as social justice, religious freedom, environmental awareness, a humane economic system, or some other social cause?

People who follow their inner wisdom and pursue a mission of social justice – I think about Thomas Merton, Dorothy Day, Dr. Martin Luther King, Jr., Rosa Parks, Gandhi, many of my Quaker Friends, and thousands of ordinary people whose names we never know – do so in a way that is directly counter to the common sense of their time and the prevailing cultural norms. Although they likely have personal friends who agree with them and a community of support, being able to act on their mission and deliver their message takes courage and a willingness to take the risk of standing against the destructive falsehoods they see in the broader community around them.

Those cultural challenges are hard to handle, and as I've found for myself, they can often arouse personal issues related to authority. However, there are other inner difficulties. There may be emotions raised by social issues – frustration, anger, a sense of injustice, and even compassion – that make it more difficult to discern the deepest truth you know and follow it. In addition, a cause may have its own language, values, and agenda that guide the statements and actions of its advocates. Being part of a group working for a cause also means that there is peer pressure to adhere to a well-defined "party line" around how to understand and respond to situations where the issue is present. Unfortunately, the leaders and most successful advocates for a particular cause are usually identified as those who are most passionate and unyielding, who vigorously impose the cause's view on the situations they are concerned about, and who inspire their supporters (and force their opponents) to see and do things their way.

So is it even possible to pursue social justice work or another type of advocacy that you passionately believe in and still be guided by your experience of the deepest truth you know?

I'd like to turn to the experience of Quakers, whose central spiritual practice is to be open to the guidance of the "inner teacher" and who also have a long history of standing for justice in the face of opposing cultural norms. For example, before mainstream society started to reject slavery and almost 200 years before Lincoln wrote the Emancipation Proclamation, some Quakers began questioning it in their own community and in society as a whole. Their anti-slavery advocacy was guided by values which they considered to be informed by the inner light, and took a long time to be effective. Nonetheless, their work against slavery was key to ending the British slave trade in 1807 and to abolishing slavery everywhere in the British empire thirty years later. In North America as well, the activities of abolitionist Quakers led many Quaker individuals and communities to free their enslaved people eighty years before the Civil War.

Why were they so successful in addressing this issue, at least compared to the United States as a whole, which didn't abolish slavery until we fought a Civil War about it almost a century later? It wasn't just that Quakers advocated against slavery, but how they went about that advocacy that led their community to make such a profound change in their understanding and support of it before much of the rest of the world.

For example, John Woolman was an abolitionist Quaker who engaged in many committed and principled activities against slavery over an extended period in the mid-1700's. He felt led to reach out to others in the Quaker community, and traveled from farmhouse to farmhouse, sharing a meal and discussing his views on slavery. As he did, he refused to eat food prepared or served by enslaved people and would insist on paying his hosts for any service he received from them. He also refused to wear clothing produced by enslaved people's labor. His statements and his actions were principled and clear, but not angry or violent. Although he was there to advocate against slavery, he delivered his message by modeling the behavior that he considered right and just. In line with his Quaker leading, he did so in a way that he felt would appeal to "that of God" within his hosts rather than convince them rationally or by passion or force. Which isn't to say that his ideas were welcomed. Woolman's statements and actions directly confronted his hosts' negative and demeaning assumptions about black people and their belief that enslaving people was essential to having a profitable business and living a prosperous life.

However, other Quaker statements and actions against slavery sometimes resembled public theater. During one Quaker meeting, abolitionist Benjamin Lay famously stood up and railed against slavery, then drew a sword and stabbed a hollowed-out Bible that had been filled with a bladder of pokeberry juice, spraying the members of the meeting with fake blood. The consensus of the meeting was that this shocking bit of drama was not in the spirit of Quaker insight and guidance by the inner light, or likely to evoke or speak to the inner light in those who witnessed it. Even so, it made a powerful statement that was widely discussed at the time and that we still remember today, 250 years later. Was Lay's dramatic, confrontational action guided by his inner wisdom? As challenging and distasteful as it was to other Quakers, he sincerely believed that it was. At the same time, it is worth noting that he did not repeat this confrontational act, even though he continued to vigorously support the abolition of slavery in other ways. With the input from other Quakers, he may have come to a deeper level of discernment about how to express his inner calling around that issue.

A question implicit in Quaker practice and in the pursuit of social justice or other causes is: How do people change in the deepest and most lasting way? Quakers would say that it is by being guided by the inner light – and I would add that it is by having an experience of the deepest truth you know. As I've seen in my own life, that experience reflects a deep sense of something being real or true. It is most reliably evoked during personal reflection or with other people in a safe and accepting interaction that doesn't impose external expectations or ideas. However, personal reflection and interactions with others exist in a social context, and there's public information about the social issues we face that is part of the material that inner wisdom is given to work with. Might someone like Benjamin Lay be inwardly guided to create a bit of theatre that becomes part of our collective discussion about a social issue? That certainly seems possible – just as someone like John Woolman might be guided to have personal interactions with others and speak to their inner light in a way that they can experience a deeper truth about an issue.

The decisions you make about whether or not to engage with a cause, and how to engage with it, clearly can be guided by your inner wisdom. There are many possibilities, dramatic and not. However, when getting involved with complex social issues with all their passions, conflicts, ideas, assumptions, language, agendas, organizations, problem-solving, and the inner and outer pressure to "do the right thing," it is all the more important to find a way to set aside these distractions to your inner wisdom and be open to guidance. From my own experience as well as what I've seen in the Quaker Friends I know who are focused on social justice issues and also open to guidance from the Light, it's hard to stay connected with inner wisdom as you get caught up in the agenda of a social cause. However, if you regularly ask for the deepest truth you know, particularly in the situations where you feel most pressured, distracted, and "right" about what you're doing, the clarity it offers can help you discern what is yours to do in that moment – and perhaps also what your mission and purpose in life needs to be.

The hidden way
The deep truth of your inner wisdom can give you the confidence to say "yes" to decisions that radically change your life and affirm your unique mission and purpose. It can also give you

the confidence to say "no" to shoes that don't quite fit, no matter how attractive they might be: the well-meaning advice you can't use, our culture's common sense about what is important, your own superficial understanding of your life, the opportunities that aren't in line with your deepest truth, and the distractions that keep you from acting on your own unique purpose. As investor Warren Buffet said, "The difference between successful people and really successful people is that really successful people say 'no' to almost everything." That also describes people who live the deepest truth they know.

Sometimes you may be led to say "no" to a hard-to-resist opportunity and not fully understand why. As I was finishing my psychology internship at Rush Medical Center, I started to look for fellowships to complete my training. As a graduate student, I had been a research assistant in the Behavioral Medicine Unit in the Strong Memorial Hospital Cancer Center in Rochester, and through my mentor and work there I had gotten to know a psychiatrist at Stanford University who studied social support in women with breast cancer. My doctoral dissertation looked at how adult attachment patterns affected social support and coping in breast cancer patients, and I had spoken to him about that project. He invited me to present my findings to his research group with the possibility, if all went well, of becoming a research fellow with him and having the opportunity to complete my clinical training.

The flight out to California was exciting, and I felt ready for my life to change yet again. And, well, it was Stanford! The presentation was successful, but strangely, I didn't feel right about it. I'd been quite comfortable and enthusiastic making other academic presentations and leading other discussions about my work, but this situation made me feel uneasy. Still, the psychiatrist invited me into his office and offered me a fellowship. I shouldn't expect to see him much when I became a fellow, he said, because he was very busy. One of his staff would arrange for me to pick up some psychotherapy clients and complete the clinical hours required to get my professional license.

All seemed fine, on the surface – and yet it wasn't fine at all. My inner alarms were going off. There was something not right about accepting that fellowship, even as prestigious as it was and as life-changing as it would be. After I returned to Chicago, I let him know I wasn't coming.

Saying "no" to that particular opportunity was difficult. A Stanford research fellowship would have set me up for an academic career anywhere I wanted to pursue one, and I remember having serious second thoughts before I refused it. I was also acutely aware that I was closing the door on a career opportunity that my research mentor at the University of Rochester had generously opened for me, and I worried about disappointing him. But as challenging as it was to turn down the fellowship, I was clear about what my inner wisdom was telling me. To be faithful to it, I simply couldn't do anything else.

A few years later, I had returned to Rush Medical College in Chicago as a faculty member and, somewhat to my surprise, found myself in the beginning stages of a research career. I'd obtained several small grants from foundations and a major one from the National Institutes of Health (NIH), published numerous articles in scientific journals, and was a member of a fascinating committee at the NIH on innovative psychosocial research in medicine. People were starting to talk with me about becoming a tenured faculty member.

But at the same time, I realized that the more successful I became as a researcher, the less I liked doing it. As much as I loved science, I didn't want to spend the rest of my life as a scientist. I didn't want to think primarily in the analytic ways that scientific inquiry required, have my closest work relationships be with other people who thought in those ways, and constantly struggle to get grants and support for my work.

I believe if I had ignored my inner wisdom and accepted the Stanford fellowship, it would have been much harder to make the decision to end my research career when it felt right to do so. Accepting that fellowship also would have probably steered me away from getting my first job as a health psychologist in Chicago, and I might never have met my wife. After refusing the opportunity at Stanford, I ended up accepting a clinical fellowship at Henry Ford Hospital in Detroit that had its own difficulties and challenges but suited me far better. I didn't fully realize it at the time, but saying "no" back then and following the deepest truth I knew in that moment made it possible for me to say "yes" to the mission and purpose I pursue now and the activities that are important to me today.

A radical "Yes"

For many people, the experience of having a mission and purpose is not about a career choice or a social cause, but about what's important in their personal life. One of the most powerful examples of this that I know occurred when my Quaker friend Kat said a particularly radical and life-changing "yes" to guidance she received after her sister tragically committed suicide. Almost immediately after she found out what had happened, without thinking it through in an ordinary way or discussing it with anyone, Kat knew that she needed to stay with her orphaned niece in Oregon for five months or so until she graduated from high school. As is often the case when you experience your deepest truth, she felt no hesitation in making that decision. Kat called her husband in Wisconsin to tell him what happened and let him know what she planned to do, and informed the school district she worked for that she wouldn't be back in the classroom until September.

"I can't really say why I was so sure that this was the absolutely right thing to do," she said. "But I never had a single regret or misgiving about it. I don't know why I lost exactly no sleep about what my employer would say, or my husband for that matter. I just *knew*. It was as simple as any decision I've ever made."

Supporting her niece in the midst of loss and grief was at the heart of Kat's decision, but she also had the onerous task of settling her sister's estate and making sure her niece received the financial support due her from the government. In the midst of the challenges, though, Kat found herself feeling something that seemed, as she put it, "wildly inappropriate." She was confused, and didn't tell anyone for a considerable time, but there it was, nonetheless: joy.

Kat didn't immediately understand her feeling. What she came to realize, however, was that her joy "was the joy of surrender, of obedience to the Spirit, and to the acceptance of grace that this surrender allows." She realized that some of the limitation she'd experienced in her personal life, her self-doubt, unworthiness, and sense of not being good enough, "was just vaporized by the simple act of obedience to what I was called to do."

When she came to fully realize this, it was an extraordinary moment. She'd just overcome a problem with her niece's Social Security claim, and to celebrate, she played Handel's "Hallelujah Chorus" at full blast and sang along. Then she got to the final line, "and He shall reign forever and ever."

"I just came completely unglued," she said. "I cried and cried." As she was crying, she was also writing a letter to her family and close friends. Here is part of what she wrote.

> *It seems so painfully ironic that my sister's final act of non-self-acceptance should have provided the opportunity for me to grow beyond my own, and yet it has. I feel remade in a deep way. I feel more whole, more healed, more deeply happy than I think I have ever felt.*
>
> *What a strange and wonderful mystery. Every day feels like a miraculous opportunity handed to me to grow deeper*

into self-acceptance, simply by doing what needs doing that day; simply by showing up and attending to the moment. The ultimate freedom and joy through nothing more than simple obedience. Why was this never accessible to me before?

So now I'm crying at the loss of my sister, and the gulf between how she felt and how I feel, and that her tragedy turned, ultimately, into my gain. I am simultaneously overwhelmed with the magnitude of what I lost in her, and the magnitude of what she lost or never had, and the hugeness of what I have somehow found. Is it even possible to cry harder than I am now for sorrow and joy at the same time?

Deep breath.

I'm not sure my heart can hold any more than it is holding right now … I think that I have just had the deepest experience of grace of my entire life – a grace so huge that it can encompass all of my sister's pain and mine and yours, and also all the joy there is.

For He shall reign forever and ever. Yup, that's about the size of it.

The memory of this joy lingers for Kat, and she describes it as one of the greatest gifts she's ever received. It did not permanently heal of her sense of unworthiness, although it gave her a "vacation from it," as she said. But it still was empowering. Her morning spiritual practice is now an exploration of "surrender, of obedience, and of the things that get in the way." There are days when she again finds joy, and she always finds new places to practice obedience to her deepest truth.

"When I do, I find that grace is usually close behind. And of course, sometimes I'm not obedient at all, and I get a kick in the butt instead," she said. "But overall, I feel a robust sense of purpose and of progress, and the proximity of a sometimes smiling, sometimes exasperated Spirit, egging me on."

When I took a "gap year" at age 34 to find a new career, I thought the process required my best intellectual self-analysis. It turned out that my mission and purpose in life appeared only when I gave up overthinking the process. I had to stop listening to the roaring wind of my own and others' ideas and expectations, and let my life find me.

SKY AND EARTH

Sky says
where I am

is somewhere
overhead

filled with
vision

gazing forward
glassy-eyed

wind
roaring

like a deafening
waterfall

Earth says
come sit

under this
green tree

eat these
warm fruits

make all sorts
of love

and don't care
so much

how you look
in the morning

Chapter 7

Welcome, Truth

We seem to know very little about creating spaces that invite the soul to show up, this core of ourselves, our selfhood.

– Parker J. Palmer

After I moved to Kansas City to explore being a writer, I met several people like myself who wanted to start a writers' group. We started with a core of three people: Charley Hammer, a former civil rights reporter from the Kansas City Star who had retired to write novels, John Wood, an accomplished advertising and marketing writer who wanted to do more personal creative writing, and me, in my early 20's with my bachelor's degree in English and the handful of poems I'd written. We were an improbable bunch for a writers' group. But even though our backgrounds and level of experience varied, we all knew how much anxiety came with reading a raw piece of writing out loud and having it scrutinized by others. So we decided to set some ground rules for our interactions that made it safe for us to share our thoughts truthfully with each other so we could become better writers.

For our first guideline, we declared that the words we put on paper were not who we were as people. Whatever we might say about the writing that members of the group shared, we respected who we were as writers and as individuals and agreed to keep feedback both honest and constructive. No matter what someone brought to read, what we said about it wasn't personal criticism. It was about the words on the page and in support of the writer.

Additionally, we'd all had the experience of groups where one or two writers, by virtue of their publications, credentials, or ego, wore the mantle of authority and always made sure they had the last word about whatever piece of writing was being considered. So our second guideline was never to stand on our academic or work credentials, life experience, professional expertise or publishing success in commenting on each other's writing. We would express our reaction to each other's work as honestly as we could as readers, not as professionals.

Those two simple ground rules for our relationship with each other in the group enabled us to not only feel safe sharing our writing, but also comfortable in sharing comments about another writer's work that were a little unconventional. For instance, one evening a writer was reading a short story to us, and I reacted in a way I didn't understand but felt I needed to share with him. "I really like what you've written," I said. "And I can keep it all fairly clear in my head, except for the first sentence. I can't remember the opening line of your story."

He stared at me for a moment. "Well," he said. "I've worked on this story for months, writing and rewriting it. The only part left from the first draft is that first sentence. I think maybe it's time to let it go."

My comment was a pretty weird thing to say, and I'm quite sure that I would never have said it in a more conventional writers' group. But it was clearly the deepest truth I knew about his story, and the safety of the group let me bring it forward. As odd as my comment may have been, it turned out to be useful to the author.

Our writers' group kept going for over thirty years, long after I left Kansas City. Most of the credit for its longevity goes to Charley and his commitment to keep the group going. But another reason it lasted so long had to do with the safe, honest, relatively ego-free relationships we created with each other to develop our craft. Our two simple guidelines – make comments about the writing, not the writer, and make comments based on your personal (not professional) response to the writing – made the group a positive presence in the Kansas City writing community for decades. Our commitment to each other's growth and excellence was deeply supportive, and our commitment to being honest without judging each other made it safe for us to speak and welcome what we felt was true about our work.

Circles of Trust

That writer's group taught me that it was possible to deliberately create safe relationships that allowed us to express honestly what we thought and felt. However, when I started to write this book, I didn't believe it was possible in a group to find and explore the more delicate promptings of inner wisdom. Even though I'd been a psychologist for over fifteen years, my own experience of receiving inner wisdom was that it was an intimate and personal process, and that group interactions wouldn't be safe enough for it. It wasn't until I read Parker Palmer's work and then experienced Circles of Trust and Clearness Committees for myself that I realized it was possible to create safe and supportive groups that allow participants to open to their inner wisdom.

As it was to a lesser extent in our writers' group, Circles of Trust make that possible by having carefully-crafted agreements about how to interact with each other. These agreements are called "touchstones." (I like that word better than "guidelines" because it energizes the process to move in a certain direction rather than putting a limit on it.) Some of these touchstones create a sense of welcome and encourage acceptance of the whole range of our human thoughts and feelings. Others preserve safety and promote a sense of inner freedom by inviting people to share and participate only when they want to, and by insisting on a deep level of confidentiality. They also encourage people to be curious about their own and other's defensive responses, and respectfully use "I" statements rather than taking on the tempting role of authority, expert or guru.

There is one "thou shalt not" in the touchstones: an admonition against fixing, saving, correcting or advising others in the group. This is vital to creating space that welcomes the soul. It is also one of the hardest touchstones to follow, especially if you're in a helping profession, as I am. As tempting as it is, providing answers to a person's questions and offering advice to solve their problems is a sure way to scare their inner wisdom into silence.

Implementing these touchstones may seem a bit cumbersome, at least initially. The first Circle of Trust retreat that my wife and I attended was at a lovely rural retreat center in Farmington, Minnesota, near Minneapolis. I remember sitting down in the circle of chairs with about twenty-five other people, a beautiful centerpiece of flowers and plants in the middle, full of anticipation. Then a few minutes after the facilitators welcomed us and provided an overview of what we would be doing for the next couple of days, we were given a densely printed single sheet of paper with eleven touchstones that we were to follow during the retreat. My heart sank as we started to read them out loud. So many rules!

As we worked through them, though, I realized that they weren't rules so much as a way of being with each other that lifted up the very best of ourselves. I also saw that they were intended to create space for honesty and genuineness. By the time we finished reading the touchstones and collectively agreed to follow them during the retreat, I remember thinking: *Yes, this is the way people should be with each other. Let's see what happens when we are.*

As the retreat continued that evening and the next day, I saw that something special was going on that I'd never experienced before – and much of it had to do with the touchstones. I also felt a leading as strong and clear as the one that led me to become a psychologist: I needed to fully understand what was happening here and make it part of my life – I needed to become a Circle of Trust facilitator myself.

Among the other unique aspects of Circles of Trust, there is one more practice I'd like to describe that beautifully makes it easier for inner wisdom to come forward. One of Parker Palmer's favorites lines of poetry is Emily Dickinson's, "Tell all the Truth but tell it slant." By exploring the truth from an angle and not directly, her wise insight is that you're likely to be less defensive and more open to receive it. As I've noted, one way to do this exploration in Circles of Trust is by looking at your question or issue through the associations and metaphors found in "third things" such as poems, stories, artwork, photos, personal objects, or nature.

For example, how does a particular aspect of your life reflect the transition of the seasons? Does that part of you relate more to Spring's reawakening and potential, Summer's fulfillment and abundance, Autumn's outward decay yet inward creation of seeds for the future, or Winter's resilient continuation and readiness for what's next? I have asked myself this particular question many times about various things happening in my life, and it always gives me a fresh understanding and appreciation for what is going on inside me.

Similarly rich insights become available when I explore the "slant" truth of other third things. For example, the poem below by William Stafford, which I encountered back in that first Circle of Trust retreat I participated in, is richly evocative for me. Every time I read it, a different phrase or line stands out and gives me insight on my inner life at that moment. A framed copy of this poem is on my waiting room wall to remind my counseling clients and others who pause to read it that there is a powerful and unique truth in each of our lives.

THE WAY IT IS

*There's a thread you follow. It goes among
things that change. But it doesn't change.
People wonder about what you are pursuing.
You have to explain about the thread.
But it is hard for others to see.
While you hold it you can't get lost.
Tragedies happen; people get hurt
or die; and you suffer and get old.
Nothing you do can stop time's unfolding.
You don't ever let go of the thread.*

– William Stafford

Open and honest questions

For me, the most transformational Circle of Trust touchstone has been, "Learn to respond to others with honest, open questions instead of counsel or corrections." Instead of asking questions to satisfy curiosity, solicit more information, or fulfill some other personal agenda of your own, it suggests you respond to others with open-ended questions that encourage them to reflect further on their experience. For example, the open and honest question, "What does this situation remind you of?" offers more potential for someone to find insight than providing your own solution to their problem. I've described these agenda-free, open-ended questions in detail as essential to the Clearness Committee process, and they are equally important in Circles of Trust.

They're not just useful in those groups, however. As a psychotherapist who has in-depth conversations with people every day, I was intrigued about what might happen if I started asking my clients open and honest questions. When I did, the first thing that I discovered was how "dishonest" I'd been as a psychotherapist. Not that I'd been untruthful or deceptive with my clients, but as a health psychologist working in medical settings where treatment goals are set and outcomes measured, I'd been trained to have a therapeutic agenda in which I would often offer advice and help my clients solve their problems.

To my dismay, when I started asking open and honest questions, I found that I had often been pursuing my therapeutic agenda in a heavy-handed way. Far more than I'd realized, I had been leaning on my clients to agree with my understanding of their problem, get to the insight I wanted them to have, or take the action that I knew would make their life better. It was painful to discover how much I was trying to manipulate my clients into being happier and healthier – and I'm sure my agenda was far more obvious to them than it was to me. I'm also sure that it sometimes led them to feel defensive and not participate as deeply in the therapy process. There were real and unfortunate consequences of keeping the steering wheel for therapy sessions firmly in my own hands and trying to drive my clients where I thought they should go.

With that uncomfortable insight about myself, I tried being less directive and asking more open and honest questions. Their responses were remarkable. My clients became more relaxed, introspective and thoughtful. They shared more of their feelings and personal thoughts, and seemed to be comfortable doing so. They were also more likely to develop a positive insight into their problems and issues. They seemed to like our work together better than they did before, but surprisingly, they gave me less credit for their progress. They were pretty sure that I wasn't doing much to help them, and that the often-profound changes they made were their own doing!

I was delighted at that, partly because it affirmed for me that inner wisdom can lead you where you need to go in your life, even during psychotherapy. But I was also glad because if a person "owns" the changes they make and doesn't see them as coming from outside themselves, they're more likely to follow through on them for the long term. It was satisfying, but ironic. I had been trained as a health psychologist to help people make lasting change to improve their health and well-being – and those positive outcomes came so much easier when I set aside my training and role as an authority and created the conditions for clients to achieve them on their own.

Clarity Sessions

After my good experience with the simple practice of asking open and honest questions of my regular clients, I decided to see if something like a Clearness Committee process could work in a one-on-one setting to help people explore their personal issues and important life decisions. Other Circle of Trust facilitators I consulted, most of whom were not therapists or counselors, generally didn't encourage it, thinking that the range and richness of questions would be greater from the multiple members of a Clearness Committee than from a single person. Even so, Parker Palmer had noted that "a circle of trust can form wherever two or three are gathered – as long as those two or three know how to create and protect a space for the soul." It seemed worth trying.

I wanted to be sure I understood what I was doing, so I tested several versions of a one-on-one process closely paralleling the format of a Clearness Committee with friends who were spiritually insightful and willing to explore this new process with me. From their detailed feedback after about eight of these "beta" sessions, it was indeed clear to me that one person asking open and honest questions wasn't quite as generative and creative a process as with several people. Nonetheless, it worked well – and it didn't require a commitment from three to five additional people to be part of the process. The ability to access inner wisdom did not depend on there being a certain number of people in the room, but on creating safe space and helping the focus person explore issues with open and honest questions.

Since that time, I've facilitated many such "Clarity Sessions" with individuals. A young woman in her early twenties had been a competitive swimmer, and for several years had been debating how to move forward in her life. A few weeks after our Clarity Session, she called me to say that she wasn't quite sure what we did during our session that made a difference, but she'd decided to apply to graduate school and get a degree in physical therapy. Another person used a Clarity Session to find a way to end his career as a financial advisor and move into a satisfying and creative retirement as a photographer. Others have addressed issues around relationships, work, finances, and even their church membership. In my experience, when a one-on-one session remains faithful to the principles and practices of a Clearness Committee, it can create space for inner wisdom in a similar way.

Welcome, truth

Circles of Trust, Clearness Committees, and Clarity Sessions all create specific relationships and interactions where you can discover the deepest truth you know about something personally important. Because people may not have experience with their inner wisdom, the process is conscious and intentional, with multiple touchstones for how to behave with others in the group and focus your own inner process. The result is wonderfully effective for most people. Although the time spent in those experiences may be short, the deep, heartfelt truth that is brought into awareness can be so significant and powerful that it affects the rest of a participant's life.

Is it possible, though, to do something simpler to create safe space for your own and another person's inner wisdom?

I have long revered the word *namaste,* a word used in the Hindu culture and by several other groups on the Indian subcontinent. Namaste is commonly used as a casual greeting between people, but it can also be used as a more serious spiritual welcoming that means, "That which is of God in me greets that which is of God in you," or "I honor the Spirit in you, which is also in me." With this intention, namaste is a reminder to the person who says it and the person who hears it that there is something possible in this moment of the relationship that is greater than casual small talk or our usual ego dance with each other. It expresses a conscious desire for the essence of one person to encounter the essence of another.

In the spirit of namaste, I've found that you can acknowledge and support another person's inner wisdom by using the phrase, *welcome, truth.* With these simple words, you are saying, "I welcome your expression of the deepest truth you know in this moment, and I am also willing to express the deepest truth I know in this moment as best I can." These two words create safety and encourage a person to turn their attention toward their genuine thoughts, feelings, and inner wisdom. You can simply tell others what you mean by that phrase, and then make it a prelude to interactions in which you want to experience deep connection and truth with them. Saying *welcome, truth* out loud lets you consciously create an open, safe place to share the deepest truth you know with each another.

You can also use *welcome, truth* as a silent affirmation, even if the other person is unaware that you're doing so. By saying it silently to yourself, you inwardly declare your intention to express your deepest truth and open yourself to the other person's truth. Doing this subtly changes your reaction to other people, and they may notice something different about you. They may see you as less defensive, and more welcoming and curious. They may perceive this in your words and actions that are in line with your intention to *welcome, truth*. They may read in your body language and facial expressions that you are relaxed, interested and receptive to them. Remember, too, that *welcome, truth* also embodies the intention of Circles of Trust, Clearness Committees, Clarity Sessions, and Quaker meetings. I have often silently said that phrase to myself during these activities to help focus my attention and purpose.

As I've experienced when I use this phrase with the people in my life, by welcoming the truth of others and letting your own truth be welcomed, your relationships take on a new depth. You can share personal experiences, support and celebrate each other's positive transformation, and explore the true places in your lives.

A deep strength

Welcoming truth in your relationship with another person doesn't require using those exact words, as a family friend of ours discovered. She'd had a conflicted relationship with her mother all her life. Her mother had always demeaned her, and she had come to dread her mother's occasional phone calls and visits. One day, however, when her mother called with some family news, she decided to turn toward a deeper truth.

Her mother was clearly angry, and perhaps resentful that she felt obligated to make the call. "Well," she said, "Your grandmother is worse and the doctors think she's dying, and your aunt's cancer has come back."

Our friend was silent for a moment, reflecting on the fact that her mother had just told her that her own mother was dying and that her sister's cancer was back. Aware that her mother was sharing something more than her usual judgments and accusations, she found herself quietly saying something she'd never said before: "How does that make you feel, Mom?"

Her mother was silent, too, and then said, "Sad. It feels really sad."

"I'm sure it does," said our friend. "Tell me more about it."

The door opened for something different in their relationship simply because our friend was willing to welcome a truth beyond the discomfort she often felt when interacting with her mother. This wasn't the end of their troubles, and by the end of the call, it didn't turn out to be a perfect conversation. But she let the door open for her mother's deeper truth to come through and for her own to be shared in return. That is how things start to change between people. As you connect with the inner peace of your true self where you no longer experience the urge to be defensive, dismissive, or avoidant, you can feel compassion and concern for the other person's pain and anger. As our friend found, the non-defensive words that naturally come out of you might be something like, "Tell me more about that" or "I'm so sorry this happened… how can I help?"

As you *welcome, truth* in relationships, you become better at accepting what is, and at letting others speak their truth – what you've done that bothers them, what they really think and feel about the situation they're in, or what they need. You become more aware of your truth as well, and have the courage and strength to speak up about what's important. As you listen with acceptance and caring to others' distress and to your own feelings, welcoming truth may move the conversation and the relationship beyond the narrow constraints of frustration and anger. That simple act with another person can help you release fear and pain, and move toward peace, freedom, and even forgiveness.

Forgiveness

The first Quaker meeting I attended was on a snowy day, and travel was difficult. I wondered whether I should wait for another time, but I'm glad I didn't. The meeting was in a beautiful older home, a cozy fire was burning in the fireplace, and the six Friends who had braved the weather welcomed me and made me feel comfortable.

For the unstructured Quaker worship where Friends sit in silent, expectant waiting for a spiritual insight or "leading," the clerk of the meeting (the person who organizes the activities) suggested a worship query: as we felt led to share, what is an experience of awe that we'd had? Then we went into silence, looking for what our inner wisdom brought forth about awe. After a while, several people described experiences they'd had in nature, and I recalled a sunset I'd seen up in Canada. Then a few minutes later, after another period of silence, I realized that in that moment, I felt awe about an experience I'd had twenty-five years earlier.

A friend and I were out walking his dog late in the evening. A car pulled over, and two young men with guns got out. They demanded we turn over our wallets. My friend resisted, was shot and went down.

Then the other young man pointed his gun at me and said, "Give me your wallet." That was the moment of greatest terror in my life, because I couldn't give him what he wanted. His partner had already taken my wallet.

I lowered my head. "I'm sorry," I said. "The other guy already took it."

Something changed in the young man's eyes. He believed me and lowered his gun. He then ran back to the car and drove away with his partner. After they left, I was relieved to find that my friend had only been wounded in the arm.

As I remembered what had happened, I became aware of something I'd never realized before: something inside the young man who had demanded my wallet made him believe me and lower his gun. Even in that moment, "that which is of God" inside him was listening to me and responded to what I said. I saw the humanity and the spirit in him, and felt awe that it was there.

At that moment, sitting quietly within a circle of Friends, something inside me forgave him and his partner. I'd long ago been able to stop thinking negatively about them and what they did, but I'd never been able to release what had happened and forgive them so that I could see them in a positive way. Only when I received the grace to recognize, with awe, the human spirit inside him was I finally able to forgive and let go of what he and his partner had done.

Then spontaneously, the question came to me: what would I do if I saw him now? I instantly realized that I wanted to tell him, "If there is anything you are burdened by or feel guilty about from that time twenty-five years ago, I hope you can let it go. I forgive you, and I hope you can go forward with your life."

I now find myself at peace about that experience so long ago. The insight I had during that Quaker meeting let me forgive the young men who traumatized and hurt me and my friend. It helped me understand how some painful relationships and experiences might can transform if you *welcome, truth* and bring them into the inner light.

I drove away from the meeting that day grateful and a bit overwhelmed. I also realized that for such a profound thing to happen at my first Quaker meeting, my inner wisdom was telling me that I should keep participating in them. Indeed, in the many Quaker meetings I've been part of since then, I've found warm friendships, kindred spirits and community. I've also become a member of the Religious Society of Friends and found a new spiritual home on my journey to live the deepest truth I know.

I wrote this poem during a retreat with a Native American friend, Larry Littlebird, of Santo Domingo Pueblo. One morning, he led us into the New Mexico hills before dawn to watch the sun rise.

WISDOM IN THE SILENCE

when I am still
everything speaks:

the black lake
before sunrise

a distant bird that calls
just once

slow air
in the desert grass

the sky brightening
behind clouds

life itself
moving

speaking
in the silence

Chapter 8
Opening to Life

My aim is not to be consistent with my previous statements on a given question, but to be consistent with truth as it may present itself to me at a given moment. The result has been that I have grown from truth to truth.

– Gandhi, Experiments with Truth

I had long wanted a family, but as I reached my late forties, my chance for getting married and having children felt as though it was slipping away. I'd been in a number of good relationships but had never felt right about getting married. Someone with my history of serial monogamy would likely be cautious about making a life-long commitment – and maybe a woman I was interested in would be understandably cautious about making a commitment to me, too. For several years, though, I'd had an image in my mind of a young girl who I somehow knew to be my daughter. I even knew her name: Katie. One day, in my inner vision I saw Katie rush over to a woman who had dark hair with sloping sides, almost like a triangle, and grab her knees. The woman bent down to hold Katie, and then she looked up at me, but I couldn't see her face clearly.

A couple of months later, I was counseling a patient on the cardiac intensive care unit at Rush Medical Center, where I was on staff as a health psychologist. In the middle of our session, the patient started to have pain radiating up her neck and to her left shoulder and upper back, which set off alarm bells in me because those sudden symptoms could mean she was having a heart attack. I called the nurse, and the nurse ran and got a physician, a critical care fellow, who turned out to be Laurin. She came in to evaluate the situation, while I tried to keep the patient as calm as I could.

I was focused completely on reassuring the patient and helping her relax, and Laurin barely registered with me when she came in the room. But thankfully, I later learned that she'd had an experience of me that she knew she had to explore. She told me later that she'd had the sensation she describes as her "sternum vibration," which is her own inner wisdom saying that something important is going on that she needs to pay attention to. After she determined that the patient's heart was fine and the symptoms were probably related to anxiety, she waited to talk with me outside at the nurses' station. But she lost her nerve and went off to see other patients before I came out of the room.

In the next few days, however, after checking me out with the nursing staff and discovering I was single and generally a nice guy, she started consulting me on patients. But I had no idea who she was at that point, so I sent the psychology interns I was supervising to see the first few patients she referred for help. After I didn't show up for the third patient she'd referred to the psychology service, she told the intern to tell me that I was "a slacker for not doing my own consults."

The intern reported this humorously rude statement to me with the grin of a co-conspirator. "You know what that means, don't you?" he said, leaning toward me. "She *likes* you!"

So I did her next referral myself, and discovered that I liked

Laurin, too. She also had dark hair, sloped on the sides like a triangle. We went out for coffee, which turned into dinner, and less than six months later, we were married. Our first daughter Katie arrived the following year.

Keeping it simple

Our relationship and marriage started off in a special way that both of us treasure, but most of my life with Laurin has seemed ordinary from the outside, even as we've both tried to stay open to a deeper truth. One night, Laurin came home late from a long day working in the intensive care unit and a long evening studying for her critical care medicine board exam. Our girls were already in bed and had been asleep for almost two hours, and Laurin was exhausted and frustrated at not seeing them.

Sitting on our couch in the living room, we talked for half an hour about the pressures of her schedule and how much she loves her job, reviewed Katie's schoolwork and Kara's dance class, told some jokes we'd heard, remembered funny things from our girls' early years, discussed getting the last bit of yard work finished before the weather turned too cold, and talked about a few more of the thousand things that make up family life. By the time we were ready for bed, she was still tired but in much better spirits – yawning but smiling.

What made Laurin's and my interaction intimate and restorative was our willingness to be with each other as fully as we could be. I didn't have an agenda to make a point about her work affecting her ability to join us for family time, and she didn't have an agenda to tell me about the household chores that I still hadn't gotten around to doing. We weren't trying to "fix, save, correct or advise" each other. What we did was create a few minutes of conscious and genuine sharing that allowed us to express the deepest truth we knew about that moment in our relationship and our lives.

Opening your whole self and putting it on the line in the present moment has great power. Bringing your whole self into the present to be with someone you love is especially powerful, and stronger than a bad day or a frustrated moment. Its power comes from the genuine connection you make that takes you beyond your distracting thoughts, feelings and pain, opening you to an experience of a deeper truth. Laurin and I were not talking about extraordinary things, but our experience of being truly present with each other made them so. What we created on that wonderfully ordinary night was an opening into greater aliveness.

The richness of now
There is a mystery about being in the present moment that goes beyond simplistic understanding. It is certainly not what you know *about* the present. It is also more than a self-conscious choice to "be in the present" with your senses and obsessively examine the beautiful colors of this flower or the lovely feathers of that bird. There is something uniquely energizing and richly textured about relaxing into the flow of the present moment that leads you into a deeper sense of reality. The deepest truth you know is the truth of the present moment and how you are aware of it and live it.

In a meditation class I sometimes teach, we do a day-long intensive session and have a "mindful potluck lunch" where everyone brings food. We each take one plate of food and do nothing for forty-five minutes but eat that food with awareness. There's no talking, no interaction with each other, and we set aside other distractions as best we can. Everyone notices things about the sensation of eating that they didn't notice before: how things crunch and chew and taste. Many people report that the food tastes absolutely wonderful, and some describe it at the best meal they've ever eaten. That "wow!" sensory experience is not so much about the quality of the food as it is about being in the present with it. The food is nothing special, but in slowing down to break the habit of unawareness, the sensory and emotional experience of eating it becomes vivid and alive.

Of course, even if you're not eating a mindful lunch, the present moment can become a way of opening to a deeper reality, a deeper truth. Being in the moment is not being spaced out or somewhere else. It's also not a desiccated, empty, exclusively sensory moment in which everything but the orange of the butterfly's wing has been stripped away. It's being as present and aware as you can be with your whole self, and letting the whole butterfly live in you. All aspects of life can open and be enlivened by this awareness – work, play, spiritual activity, family and friends. Opening to the truth creates an experience that is rich and full.

Practicing new habits

In my meditation class, I often ask the participants, "What have you been practicing?" By this, I mean for all of us to look at our habitual ways of being and doing in the world. Perhaps if you ask yourself that question, you notice that you've been practicing impatience or irritability. Maybe you've been focusing on how right and self-satisfied you are, or how wrong and self-doubtful you are. Maybe you've been practicing generosity and gratitude, peacefulness and kindness, or just calmly staying in the moment. As you look at the ways of being and doing that you've been practicing, the point is not to judge some practices as good and some as bad, but to become aware of what you're practicing and see how it relates to your life experience and the deepest truth you know.

Becoming aware of how you engage with yourself, others and the world is important. Your habits of heart and mind create a way of understanding what's around you and who you are. Most of the time you may unconsciously react with thoughts and feelings that reflexively define who you are and what you think the world is about. Someone cuts you off in traffic, and you get enraged at their arrogance and obsessed with your own victimhood. Someone you love dies, and it's hard to stay present in the moment: maybe you're sad, lonely and angry with them for leaving you, or totally focused on what needs to be done for the funeral and not feeling anything at all. Or a politician makes a statement, and you find yourself holding that person in disgusted contempt or exalted admiration.

These habits of the heart and mind create the texture of your feelings and thoughts that you live with and share with others, and they become part of the identity you take on in the world. They may seem natural and inevitable, a deep part of who you are. It often comes as a surprise to discover that your habits of heart and mind are not fixed and unmovable character traits, and that changing them is often simply a matter of starting a regular practice of new, more consciously intentional habits. In my work as a psychologist with heart patients, I've met with hundreds of people who considered their "Type A" behavior (their hard-driving, goal-oriented cynical hostility) to be unquestionably a part of who they were and would always be. Nonetheless, with a commitment to mindful practice, relaxation, and new ways of being, many of them discovered that they could change their Type A behaviors in just a few months and become kinder to themselves and more caring about the other people in their lives.

As you become more aware of the inner and outer pressures to be something other than yourself, you often discover that you can relax and not be so concerned about how you think others see you. For instance, my friend Bill started teaching yoga about six years ago.

"Initially, I was nervous about getting it right," he said. "For a long time, I put a lot of effort into thinking through which positions I wanted to use in each class and the order to present them. I also outlined everything I wanted to say."

Even with all his preparation, however, he didn't feel that he was doing a good job teaching. "There were people with a wide range of experience in each class. Some were beginners and some had been doing yoga for years. I could never figure out how to teach everyone, and it was frustrating. And not just for me – from the reactions of the students, I could tell that I was sometimes literally just going through the motions and not teaching anybody."

Then he realized that he was practicing a very limited way of teaching based on his fear of making a mistake and not looking good. His old habits of heart and mind were getting in the way, and he knew there had to be another approach. He started to practice being mindful of the people in the class and how they responded to what he was asking them to do.

"Instead of trying so hard to get everything right, I began to pay attention to how people were responding to the postures I asked them to do," he said. "Maybe someone was straining and I could talk about easing into a pose. I started to let the sequence of postures and what I said about them flow naturally from the student's experience."

Beginners and advanced students alike began telling him how much they enjoyed his classes, and people started seeking him out as an instructor. His level of satisfaction in teaching and his trust in himself increased.

"I used what I learned in teaching yoga at my work, too," he said. "Previously, when I made a presentation to my staff or to the upper-level managers in my company, I'd scripted and memorized every word I wanted to say. I got the information out, but it always felt awkward. Then I started making a list of one- or two-word topics to make sure I remembered what I wanted to talk about and just spoke from my heart. It made a huge difference."

Less is sometimes more, particularly when you feel that it's necessary to rationally think through everything that's needed to get the job done. Often the purpose of such thinking is less about doing good work and more about feeling in control and reducing your anxiety about criticism or failure. But when you're engaged with the situation so you can discern and act on what's right for you and others, you're in touch with a deeper truth that lets you respond easily and without thinking about it. When Bill let go of his worry about making mistakes and started practicing being aware of his students' experience and the deepest truth he knew in the moment, his teaching became easier and more satisfying for everyone.

Growing from truth to truth

As Gandhi experimented with the deepest truth he knew about political and economic freedom in India and nonviolent ways of change, he saw that over time he grew "from truth to truth." That expansive, generous way of opening to the deepest truth you know, without getting stuck on "the Truth" as an ultimate destination, allows you to expand your perspective on what is real and true as your life inevitably grows and changes.

As you get older, you often can't do the things that were possible when you were in your teens and 20s. I played soccer in high school and college and for several years afterwards, but now, in my late sixties and having had my painfully arthritic knees surgically replaced, I know that I will never again race down a soccer field and loft a perfectly timed cross into the center of the field to a teammate in front of the opponent's goal.

There's some nostalgic regret for me in that, but it's trivial compared to facing a life-changing illness or physical problem that keeps a person from doing things that are essential and important to them. Changes of that magnitude may end someone's ability to work, disrupt their financial security or alter their established role in their family. Sooner or later, however, everyone encounters limits to their abilities. Part of your life's inner work, and the work of attending to your inner wisdom, is to discover how to live fully and well within those limits.

How graceful people are at accepting change varies a lot. When I was training to be a psychologist, one of my clients decided that turning fifty was the most terrible thing he could imagine. He was convinced that his life would be all downhill from there. He couldn't see anything in front of him except health problems, restrictions to his lifestyle, and increasing limits on his physical abilities and activities. Facing what seemed to him a bleak future, he wanted to kill himself. Despite being in reasonably good health and having a family, a meaningful job, and even a cabin in the woods where he could go to be in nature whenever he wanted, he could see nothing in his present life or his future that justified him continuing to live.

The question he faced (and thankfully was able to find a positive answer to) is the same that confronts everyone: What makes life worth living? Most people have experienced that what they find worthwhile in life doesn't stay the same over time. But life is not a superficial story about the empty finding and losing of experiences, possessions, and relationships – or at least it doesn't have to be. As you personally grow from "truth to truth," it can be about opening yourself in the most meaningful way you can, whatever may come your way and however your circumstances and relationships may change.

When she was eighty-six years old, my mother had to move from her apartment in Toledo, Ohio, the city where she'd lived for most of her life, to an assisted living facility in Wisconsin where she could be close to me and my family. As my sister helped her pack up what she needed from the apartment she'd lived in for twenty-five years, she was glad to let go of mere "things."

"Throw all that stuff out!" she said. "Or sell it. They're just *things*. All I need is a few suitcases."

When she got to Wisconsin, she made the very best of the

change. She was delighted to be near her granddaughters, pleased with the assisted living support she received where she was living, and genuinely intrigued at the prospect of making new friends. She kept up her routine of walking about thirty minutes a day and keeping as fit as she reasonably could. She ate in a healthy way, kept her weight down, and made sure her mind stayed active with reading and from being involved with people she could support and enjoy. She even started a book club.

It wasn't easy, though. Although my mom was healthier in most ways than people half her age, she still had a few medical problems. She started to pass out frequently and needed a pacemaker. Perhaps the most frightening thing for me as her son was seeing subtle changes in how her memory and her mind worked. I worried about what would happen to her as the years went by. Would she be able to keep her memory and ability to concentrate? And what if she couldn't?

Psychologists can be nosey about personal matters, and I asked her what it would be like for her if her memory and concentration started to go. Her response was typically thoughtful, but surprising nonetheless.

"I don't know what that would be like," she said. "But I'm sure that whatever the end of my life brings, it will be an adventure."

Of all the gifts she's passed on to me, that's the one I treasure the most. At the time, when I was working intensively with medical patients, I thought of what she said as perhaps the ultimate statement of health. Health is not just staying alive, or even living an active life, but making whatever your experiences may be into a life-giving adventure.

Years later, I now understand what she said as a statement of the deepest truth she knew. Experiences, identities, possessions, money, and relationships come to you, and then change. Life is the adventure of enjoying them while they're here, letting them go when the time is right, and then opening your life and your heart to what's next. It's certainly a rare person who can do this in all areas of life, and no one does it all the time, but that is how you live the deepest truth you know.

Letting go with grace

On the day that I planned to start writing this chapter, my mother had a severe stroke. I sat by her hospital bed, holding her hand, touching her forehead as she breathed laboriously. When my sister and I said her name and told her we loved her, she sometimes responded by turning her head and looking at us blankly for a few seconds, and then she would drift away. I am not sure she knew we were there, or whether she was just responding to the sound of our voices. Yet there was a beauty in her face, something that transcended her elderly physical body.

Six days later, her consciousness moved on and completed the process of letting go of this world. I am grateful to have spent the last two nights of her life with her in her apartment. She died while I was asleep, sometime not long after 2:00 a.m. when she seemed stable and I had gone into the next room to take a nap. A hospice worker kindly told me that people sometimes choose how they die, and if she'd wanted me sitting with her when she passed on, that's how it would have happened. She was always a modest and private person, and that is how she died – in her own way, by herself.

I became aware of many things in my mother's final days and afterwards. The acceptance and support that we had offered each other as we both got older allowed me to feel a sweet sadness at her passing and gratitude for her life, not just the pain of her loss. What I appreciated most was her positive influence and presence. Her adventurous outlook, artistic sensibility, love of nature, encouragement of other women, appreciation for new experiences, and unwavering support of my sister and me still infuse the experience of everything I do.

My mother's death, and the relationship I was able to have with her toward the end of her life, made it clear to me that the deepest truth you know gives you an honest and real place to stand in your closest relationships. As you consciously connect what is true in you with what is true in others, it gives you the confidence and strength to create relationships that reflect who you really are. It opens you to greater love and acceptance of others as you each change and grow, and as your relationships come to their natural end.

This is another prose poem from my college years. Even then, I knew that my relationship with "the deep thing" inside me was profoundly important, and that I needed to welcome its truth.

WATERTOWER

A watertower is like a silver egg in its nest of trees. You can imagine some of the hatchlings: tea holders, toilet floats, depth charges.

But what really lives inside the steel walls? Lynch mobs with flashlights, radio-controlled planes, and desperate salmon with, at last, no place to go and facing death,

the beauty of it, the relief, the crying, the deep thing floating up and breaking through.

For it rises slowly and bursts slowly and showers down the silver water of evening.

And what is within approaches through the air.

And one you've always loved within yourself awakens and says, *Here it is, it's come for you – and I'm going too, we'll go together.*

And you drift out with it through the trees and into the evening.

Chapter 9

Fully Alive

For the glory of God is a human being fully alive, and being fully alive consists of beholding God.

– St. Irenaeus, 2nd century A.D.

As I start writing this final chapter, a candle softly illuminates my desk. The candle holder is a round piece of birch wood, beautifully turned and stained light brown by First Nation artist Rand Tapper from North Bay, Ontario. Dark curved lines around open spaces in the wood remind me of ancient maps of unexplored territories. A natural radiance extends from the top to the bottom, almost as if the light from the candle flame moves into and through the wood.

Most prominent, though, is a dark place, a deep rift in the wood filled with bark where the tree attempted to heal itself after a break. I think of the healings I saw over the decades when I was active as a clinical health psychologist and psychotherapist, the deep hurts in people's lives that became part of something larger and stronger as they moved forward. I'm grateful to have witnessed and been part of their healing and growth.

The candle isn't the only source of light in my office where I write, of course, since I usually turn on other lights in the room. Furthermore, a computer sits in front of me. The bright computer screen and the other lights in the room can easily make the light of the candle seem unnecessary and irrelevant, at least as far as the practical needs of a writer are concerned.

Even so, it's important to me that the candle is there, adding its gentle glow. Its subtle flickering warmth, which I can feel on my face if I pay close attention to it, is alive in a way that feels familiar and comforting. The candle is breathing with me, metabolizing oxygen and wax to create heat and light just as I metabolize oxygen and nutrients inside my body to stay warm. We have, in our way, a kinship to each other that I don't have with my computer screen, no matter how informative and interesting what I see on that screen might be.

The candle is important to me in another way, too: it helps me remember that there are alternatives to the way we usually see and do things. It reminds me of another phrase that's often used in the same way as I use the words *inner wisdom.* The candle's gentle presence represents the *inner light,* the spirit within that is authentic, real and alive. It reminds me of the difficulties we all face to keep our inner light in view, and the challenging and sometimes painful journey we're on to make the inner light our guide in daily life.

My own journey in this book began with the story of a young man who was frightened and unsure of himself. To keep a positive sense of himself alive and start to explore who he was, he held on desperately to the deepest truth he knew at the time, which was that he was a writer. Although he had some remarkable experiences when he acted on his inner wisdom, there was, and still is, nothing particularly special about that man. I still have anxieties and fears, automatic and unskillful reactions that interfere with my relationships and my ability to do the things I want to do, and a tragicomic inability to keep my workspace organized. Yet perhaps more than most people, I've chosen to follow a deeper truth when it's been available to me, and my life has been richer and more meaningful as a result.

Thankfully, living the deepest truth you know is not something that's possible only for people who are unusual or gifted, free from financial worries or personal problems, well organized, dedicated to a spiritual practice, or who have lived long or suffered much. This is a way forward for anyone who wants to use it to make important life decisions – and it is a way to live for anyone willing to commit their life to it. The opportunity to live the deepest truth you know is a gift, a part of your human heritage. You can start wherever you are and take one step at a time.

Common humanity

I've learned a lot from the people around me who have done their best to follow the deepest truth they know in their own way, even if they would call it something like "doing the right thing" or "just trying to be happy." Sometimes they struggle with knowing their deepest truth, and sometimes it's hard to act on. But where they succeed, they nearly always describe those parts of their life as the places where they are the most successful, happy, and fulfilled.

My friend Steve and I have known each other since seventh grade. He's done some remarkable things in his life to stay faithful to the deepest truth he knows in his career and his personal life. With his undergraduate degree in chemistry, he found a position as a junior research chemist and helped me get a job weighing out chemicals from large containers into small ones. But he wanted to be more than a junior research chemist. He applied to graduate school and spent two years at Stanford, where he studied aquatic geochemistry, the chemistry of the interaction between rocks and minerals and the natural waters in streams, rivers, lakes, and the ocean.

He was interested in his studies but stopped with a master's degree because he saw that getting a Ph.D. would channel him into industry or an academic career, neither of which he wanted. He dropped out of his doctoral program, shaved his head and promised himself that he would start growing his hair again only when he knew what he wanted to do with his life. With his shaved head and his question about what he should do with himself, he moved to Madison, Wisconsin and worked for several years in a natural foods and tofu co-op.

While he was there, he decided that what he really wanted to do was teach science in a more practical way to the vast majority of teenagers in high school who weren't going to take science courses in college. So he went back to school to study education, get a teaching certificate, and let his hair grow out. His first teaching job was at a prestigious private school in Chicago. He soon realized, however, that he was essentially teaching in a college prep program, and his particular perspective on making science meaningful to students who were not college-bound wasn't as relevant there. Following the deepest truth he knew, he moved on to teach chemistry and math at public schools in Milwaukee, both in the inner city and the suburbs.

Over the years, Steve started an astronomy club at his school so that city kids could learn something about the night sky that they could barely see from their urban location. He chose to take the bus to work, which enabled him to meet informally outside of class with many of his students who also took the bus. He started a backpacking and rock climbing club for his students. He built an electric truck, and included his students in the process.

Then after many years, he officially "retired" from teaching. "Actually, I left to open up to new missions as a teacher – and I've found them," he said.

He took the few weeks off required by the retirement clauses in his teaching contract and then found another teaching job. "Nobody else wanted it," he told me. It was a job teaching science and chemistry at one of the most difficult inner city schools in Milwaukee. The year before, the class had been taught by a substitute teacher for the entire year.

"I'm doing it out of a commitment and as payback," he said. "My girls got a wonderful education in Milwaukee public schools, and it's my 'thank you' for what they received. This new job is very challenging, very intense, but I'm making progress. What I do is important, and my deepest truth goes into my work. I'm putting myself into situations that mean something to me, and I feel good about it."

As long as I've known him, Steve's commitment to his career and his family has reflected the deepest truth he knows. His path has taken the simple form, *Be true to yourself*. He's paid attention to what matters to him and what he needs, and has done his best to make sure he has those things in his life. He's far from perfect and not always happy, but he's avoided most of the major distractions that can derail your attention and rob you of time: drugs, alcohol, money, striving for status and success, possessions, gossip, meaningless relationships, and excessive involvement with the Internet and television. He lives the deepest truth he knows without making a big deal out of it.

Steve has a sense of vitality and engagement with the people in his life and what he's doing. People around him feel that he's a real person. That's perhaps his greatest gift to his students, showing them that there are adults who are true to themselves and opening the door to the possibility that as they become adults, they can be true to themselves, too.

Ordinary miracles

About twenty-five years ago, my wife Laurin was preparing for a career as a primary care doctor in internal medicine and finishing up her medical residency in Milwaukee. One afternoon after she'd finished her shift and was walking to her car, she suddenly got the urge to apply for fellowships in critical care medicine, which involves working with very ill patients in intensive care units. She'd never thought of doing that before and it was quite different than practicing primary care outpatient medicine, but it somehow made perfectly good sense to her. Against her academic advisor's advice, she felt moved to apply to only one fellowship – and she was accepted in the prestigious critical care program at Rush Medical Center in Chicago. She later found that there had been more than seventy applicants for four fellowship positions. She was challenged by the work but enjoyed it very much and has made a career out of it. She met me there, too, and we both believe that part of the reason she was led to Rush was so that she and I could create a life together.

My experience in discovering the book *Medicine as a Human Experience* had a similar unexpected flavor to it. The moment I saw the book's title, I felt a sense of recognition and was drawn to it. That response originated from a deep place within myself where I was actively living the question of what I should do next in my life. The ideas in the book resonated with me, and I knew with both passion and certainty that I needed to explore them further by going back to graduate school and becoming a psychologist.

When I talk with people about how they make their most important life decisions, there's often an element to the process that doesn't make sense in the ordinary way. A college student knows there's a glut of teachers in the market and few jobs available at the moment, but she follows her heart, gets her teaching certificate and then has a rewarding career as a teacher. A young man and woman have a deep connection that they know is more than teenage passion, fall in love and get married despite resistance from both of their families, and have a fine marriage. An older couple is drawn to move to a part of the world they've never been, and their new life in that place gives them rich experiences and insights into what's important to them.

That's how it's worked for me, too, as I've shared in my stories. It's happened more recently, too. After I moved from the private cardiology practice where I'd worked for eight years into my own office, I had a seductively distracting idea similar to the one I'd had long ago when I completed the Civil Service exam and received a job offer from the Social Security Administration. Instead of continuing to work, I thought, maybe I was ready for retirement. I started thinking about the options that American males seem to focus on when considering early retirement: getting more into my hobbies, reviving a nearly dormant golf game, or perhaps taking a cooking class. But after a few days, I realized that retirement wasn't for me, at least not then. I get bored when I spend more than an hour at the beach, and I couldn't imagine giving up the possibility of helping people. I also had a growing sense that I wanted to be a guide for people who wanted to live the deepest truth they know.

But besides writing this book, which I'd started a few months earlier, how could I go forward with what I felt called to do? What my inner wisdom brought into my awareness was that I needed a major project – a twenty-year project – to occupy me from my mid-fifties into my mid-seventies. I started to list ideas about how I could help individuals work with their inner wisdom. But not long after I started that list, my inner wisdom wanted me to do something more important first. These words came to me:

When you decide who you want to be, what there is for you to do will become clear.

A lot happened after that as I shifted my focus from what I thought I should do to deciding who I wanted to be. The main insight came when I felt guided to read the work of Parker Palmer and realized that exploring inner wisdom wasn't limited to individual contemplative practice but could be part of an intentional group process. As I've described, about an hour into the Circle of Trust retreat in Minnesota that my wife and I signed up for, I realized that I needed to become a retreat facilitator and work with groups of people to facilitate their discovery of the deepest truth they know.

What I discovered during the two-year program of facilitator preparation to lead Circles of Trust wasn't what I expected, though. Yes, facilitator preparation was about learning to do what it takes to lead retreats, but more importantly, it was about preparing a facilitator to be a certain type of person. What kind of person is that? After a few months in the program, with the excited sense of having cracked a secret code, I realized that the touchstones for a Circle of Trust retreat not only give guidance for the actions of retreat participants, but beautifully describe the ways that facilitators need to be: welcoming, invitational, present, respectful, safe, willing to wonder, unwilling to advise or correct, trusting in each person's process, and above all, focused on what we hear from our "shy soul," our inner teacher.

Now it was clear: I wanted to be, or try to be, that person, both inside and outside the retreat setting. Following those touchstones, and with the guidance of wonderfully insightful mentors, I started down a path that would let my actions, and my sense of myself and others, arise from that way of being.

I'm not always successful at this, of course. It's hard to set aside life-long intellectual ways of thinking, unhelpful emotional responses, and the limits of my professional role in the world. But it's a transformational challenge that I choose to embrace with the trust and courage needed to let it guide me where I need to go.

What I've found in doing so is that when you open to the deepest truth you know, you're given the opportunity to be present to life with all your humanity. Simply put, the fact that your inner wisdom exists shows that it is the nature of human beings to be informed and guided by something deeper than your usual thoughts and feelings. This ordinary miracle of your inner wisdom is a real and true part of who you are, an integral aspect of your nature. When you finally come to respect that truth, you can set aside many of your assumptions about the world and your place in it. You can let go of the fears that confine you to living only a fraction of who you are. As you do, the deepest truth you know will guide you beyond your personal and cultural limitations and lead you home.

One with your deepest truth

As you begin to treasure the insights that come when you ask for your inner wisdom, you may still feel that you're on the outside, looking in. Early on, it's as if you're asking a wise and respected advisor for directions: the very process of asking acknowledges that your deepest truth is somewhere other than where you are. As you continue to ask for the deepest truth you know, however, it becomes familiar and even ordinary, something that you identify with and consider part of yourself. What might it be like, then, to align so closely with your inner wisdom that, at least sometimes, your experience of the deepest truth you know is seamless with who you are and what you experience in daily life?

When you genuinely welcome and embrace the deepest truth you know at that deep level, you close the gap between your inner wisdom and yourself. When you reach this new level of acceptance, you lose your self-consciousness about asking for the deepest truth you know or welcoming others' truth. At this level, your relationship with your inner wisdom becomes like your best relationships with friends and family members: you can simply relax into it and let it be seamless with who you are. You're so comfortably engaged with your deepest truth that it becomes a simple thing to act on it. You begin to live the deepest truth you know.

Both obvious and subtle signs will show that you're living your deepest truth. For one thing, you may feel more energized. When you set aside your battle against the ideas, beliefs and identity that society imposes on you or that you struggle with inside yourself, you have more energy to be engaged with what you truly care about. You start to experience a subtle, authentic sense of who you are, and a quiet confidence and strength that accompanies that clear sense of being. As you become comfortable with what you find most true and real, you can better handle the challenges that the world brings your way.

That inner sense of strength and identity also affects your relationships with others. People can be a great joy – but from our ego's perspective, sometimes they're our greatest threat. Standing in the deepest truth you know, you discover that you aren't endangered by the thoughts and feelings of people you disagree with. You know that others can't hurt anything real about who you are, and you can welcome their truth and your own. As you act in line with your inner wisdom to speak or be silent, get involved or do nothing, make a relationship closer or more distant, who you are with other people becomes more authentic and real. Nothing is more alive than a relationship that exists because of each person's commitment to the deepest truth they know.

Accepting life

Living the deepest truth you know is like learning how to light a fire in the snow. You have to manage the environment inside yourself that at any moment is ready to extinguish your flame. You have to be careful with your attention, time and resources so that they support and not interfere with your inner wisdom. That means making good decisions about how you occupy yourself, how you interact with others, and what you turn toward and turn away from. On behalf of your inner wisdom, you need to become a good steward of your inner life.

Over the course of this book, I've tried to show that there is a simplicity in this way of living and in seeing things directly, as your inner wisdom shows them to you. As simple as it may be, though, there is nothing passive about it. Choosing to live the deepest truth you know often poses a serious challenge to the conventional truths you think you must follow. That sense of challenge may persist or evolve, and actively require you to resist falling back into old ways – perhaps for the rest of your life. But once your inner and outer resistances begin to let go, you can affirm and appreciate the remarkable ways that life shows up around you and in you. You can develop a fearless compassion and humble assertiveness with other people that allows you to speak your truth confidently, act with integrity, and connect more deeply with life.

The pattern of resistance and letting go happens over and over as you live the deepest truth you know. It was there in my experiences of discovering myself as a writer early in my life, and when I moved from one city to another with nothing more than the inner certainty that the new city was where I needed to be. I felt inner doubts and conflict when I was guided to places to live, to work that let me make a living doing what I loved, and to a mission in service to medical patients and the medical community. I struggled to change myself when I was led to become the person I needed to be as a Circle of Trust facilitator, and to help others live the deepest truth they know.

Nonetheless, to follow this path is to let your inner light open you into the person you truly are. To paraphrase St. Irenaeus' quote from the second century that begins this chapter:

There is glory in being fully alive as who you really are –
and being fully alive is to live the deepest truth you know.

It takes nothing more, or less, than trusting and being faithful to the living truth that guides you. Don't underestimate the difficulty of this. Life has a way of keeping you on the edge of what you haven't quite mastered yet. Furthermore, the insights you receive from your inner wisdom will evolve and change, just as you will. The deepest truth you know about your work and the issues you face in your personal life will certainly not be the deepest truth you live next year, or perhaps even tomorrow, if you pay attention to how it lives in you. Thankfully, the task is simple: to welcome your deepest truth about what's important to you and let your heart and actions be guided by it. The gift you receive is a life you can be grateful and satisfied to have lived.

> *When it's over, I want to say: all my life*
> *I was a bride married to amazement.*
> *I was a bridegroom, taking the world into my arms.*
>
> – Mary Oliver, from "When Death Comes"

When you follow your inner wisdom, you become fully alive to the energy and vitality of life that is yours to enjoy and to share. As you do, your inner knowing fills the present moment, and then empties with acceptance, compassion, and grace. Your life breathes, and you speak with your own voice and act with integrity, faithful to your truth. You live the deepest truth you know and become the deepest truth you are.

To end, let me say that I am still amazed and blessed by how natural it felt to follow the deepest truth I know and turn 48 years of bachelorhood into a loving marriage. This poem is about the first photograph taken of Laurin and me together, at the wedding of her cousin a few months after we met.

FIRST PHOTO

– for Laurin

Your face and mine, as if they'd always been
together, smiling side by side
in photos all our lives.

But no, this is the first – we've just begun
recording moments as we walk
together on our path

of life in love, and the great mystery
that brings souls meant to be as one
to stand as we do, strong

and confident, in front of a stone church
where two young folk have also linked
their lives as we will soon

in love. So here we stand, embracing, arms
around each other's heart and soul
for now and for all time

eternally present in this moment
yet ready to move on, eyes bright
in quiet joy.

Appendix

Your Own Journey

The spiritual journey is individual, highly personal. It can't be organized or regulated. It isn't true that everyone should follow one path. Listen to your own truth.

– Ram Dass

As I've found in my own life, you don't know all the reasons why you're on your particular journey in life, where your travels might take you, or what you might discover on the way. What may be clear, however, is that there's something inside you, nudging you along – and that you need to respond to it and take action. In my case, what was essential was following my inner wisdom, writing to discover who I was, and a lot of personal healing and growth. Your own path is sure to be uniquely yours, as Ram Dass says.

If you've read this far, though, perhaps you're thinking that part of your path might involve connecting with your inner wisdom and learning to live the deepest truth you know. If that's true for you – good!

Actually, I hope you've already tried to do that. Maybe you've done a "gut check" about a situation you were in, tried to feel where your heart was leading you when you were making a decision, or just decided to sleep on a problem and see what insight you had about it in the morning. Or perhaps you've prayed about it and asked for an answer to come to you. Maybe you've attended a Circle of Trust retreat or a Quaker meeting for worship that encouraged you to be aware of your inner teacher or the inner light. You might have tried asking directly for the deepest truth you know about a question or issue you're dealing with. You could have practiced saying *welcome, truth* either silently or out loud with a friend. Or perhaps you simply tried to follow the idea that my wife has found so useful: *Find the deepest truth you know and let everything else fall in place around it.*

Even though there are things you can do to find your inner wisdom, how to become aware of the deepest truth you know is more challenging than it might seem. It's not a simple "how to," with a series of clear steps that will immediately open that door. In fact, your answer to this question may be the answer to another, more difficult one: What personal and spiritual challenges do you need to deal with to become your true self? You're not so much reading a map to find where the treasure is hidden, but seeing where the path goes and how you need to grow and change in order to take your next step.

Still, as you discover and address your personal challenges, you can do things to make your inner wisdom's guidance part of your path. I want to share a brief outline of five activities that can help you become aware of your inner wisdom. You can fill in the details of each activity from the stories and examples in this book, as you find that they are relevant to your life and resonate with you. You'll find that they're not necessarily sequential activities – they may occur and reoccur in different orders as you work with them. Feel free to focus on the processes that work best for you at evoking your inner wisdom.

How these activities work will depend on where you are in

your life and how awareness of inner wisdom can help you move forward. Be patient with yourself. It's more important to be on the journey than to travel in a particular way. I hope you'll approach this work with curiosity and see what you discover.

1. Engage with a personal question or issue you care deeply about.

Usually, before your inner wisdom will reveal itself, you need to be engaged with a meaningful problem or question at a deep level. It might be a career choice you're considering, a relationship you're challenged by, or a life issue you're dealing with. This usually isn't comfortable, as you know. You may find the process frustrating or challenging, or feel forced to address the issue. Or you may find that it arises in you out of a deep unfulfilled need. Sometimes your engagement is a conscious process: even if the issue raises a lot of emotions, I find that it's often helpful for me to find out what I think I need to know about it before I ask for guidance from my inner wisdom about a direction to take. On the other hand, even in the midst of your struggle, by welcoming truth or the inner light you may unexpectedly find an insight coming forward. Either way, it nearly always seems that when your inner wisdom has something to say, it's about something important to you.

2. Let your perspective on it grow or change.

As you deeply engage with your question or issue, you may find that your current perspective it isn't useful in understanding what's going on or deciding what to do. So a second part of becoming aware of your deepest truth is to open yourself to different ways of looking at it. This may mean creating a time and space for silent reflection, using a third thing to inspire a different perspective, taking a break (maybe going for a walk or "sleeping on it"), or discovering something new about it beyond what you already know. In my own life, it often means deliberately taking on a "yes, and…" attitude. I frequently ask myself: What else could be going on here? My inner wisdom usually has an answer to that question.

3. Expect – or ask directly – for the deepest truth you know.

As you become deeply engaged and explore different perspectives on your question or issue, insight may come to you. Look for it and expect it. But at some point, it may also feel right to ask directly for the deepest truth you know. Remember that when you do this (that is, when you literally and sincerely say to yourself, "What is the deepest truth I know about…?" or when you explore it with a third thing, a Clearness Committee, or some other process), you declare that you're open to something more than an ordinary, rational solution to your problem. As you do, you set the intention that you'll become aware of a deeper truth. You also surrender your certainty and preconceptions about what you think you know, which offers your inner wisdom the opportunity to come forward.

4. Be open and accepting of the response that comes.

After inwardly asking for the deepest truth you know, let yourself be open to what happens next. This may be something surprising or unexpected: words, images, a feeling, or just a heightened awareness. Remember that your inner wisdom comes from a loving and true place inside you that takes into account more than the situation or problem as you define it or understand it. It responds to a larger truth about who you are and what you need, even if that way of thinking about yourself and your needs isn't apparent to you in the moment. In doing this, inner wisdom connects you with a reality greater than what you consciously know. As a result, what comes forward may be larger and more encompassing – or smaller and more personally relevant – than you expect.

5. Discern whether it's really true for you.

A final activity in becoming aware of your inner wisdom is to discern whether it's the "real thing." Is what you believe to be your inner wisdom really the deepest truth you know, or is it something else, such as your usual thoughts, feelings, or beliefs? Sometimes the answer is obvious because of the deep sense of truth or surprise that an insight evokes in you. Or the insight may express a kindness and compassion that's easy to identify as your inner wisdom. At other times, perhaps when you're experiencing inner conflict or are not sure what your inner wisdom is telling you, it's not so clear. Discernment may require patience and perspective, or perhaps a conversation with a wise companion to help you explore it more deeply. Developing the self-awareness to discern your deepest truth is at the heart of being able to act confidently on the insight it offers you.

*May you find the trust, courage, and clarity
to live the life that's truly yours.*

Gratitude

I'm profoundly grateful for everyone who has helped me learn about living the deepest truth you know. In particular, I want to raise up Parker Palmer for his wisdom, insight, and generous heart, for developing the Circle of Trust® practices, and for offering his personal guidance and insights during my facilitator preparation process and afterwards. I also want to thank my spiritual brother and friend Dr. Jerry Epps, who has been a deep and wholehearted part of my life journey for over forty-five years. He and I still support each other and regularly share what we're discovering on the path. Both Parker and Jerry are remarkable examples of people who live the deepest truth they know.

In addition, I'd like to warmly thank the other extraordinary people I've been challenged and inspired by from the Center for Courage & Renewal, especially my very patient mentor during Circle of Trust facilitator preparation, Wint Boyd. Grateful thanks and deep respect also go to Marcy and Rick Jackson, Marianne Houston, John Fenner, Sally Zare, Judy Brown, and Laura Kinkead, who all played an important role in my learning. A special thanks goes to fellow facilitator Judy Rose, who touched a deep part of my soul by introducing me to the Native American flute and then generously gifting me one of her own. I'd also like to thank my favorite Circle of Trust facilitators from the UK:

Barbara Reid, who invited me to co-facilitate with her during an important time in my learning, and Nick Ross, whose friendship, insight and support I've valued for many years, even before he became a facilitator.

I want to thank my wife Laurin, Kat Griffith, Lori Yadin, Bill Santoski, Kelly Harmelink-Keck, my psychotherapy clients, and my life-long friend Steve Marshall for their personal stories of living the deepest truth they know. I also appreciate being able to include the dramatic and insightful stories of Elizabeth Gilbert, Joe McMoneagle, and Vontae Davis about how they followed their inner wisdom. I particularly want to thank Kat for welcoming me into the Winnebago Friends Worship Group, which has become an important part of living the deepest truth I know.

Many people helped with the practical aspects of creating this book. Deep thanks to my tireless and devoted friends, family and colleagues who offered their reactions to the manuscript and helped it become far better, most notably my wife Laurin and my friends Joe Roscoe, Janet Stratton, Kat Griffith, Jonathan Elmer, Jeanne Loehnis, Eric Roycraft, Barbara Loots, and Nick Ross. Editor extraordinaire Sheryl Fullerton generously reviewed an early draft of the book and made many helpful suggestions. My copy editors Jane Salisbury and Jennie Cohen worked their magic and made the text more focused and easier to read.

Finally, I'd like to offer special thanks to my lovely wife and talented fellow author, Laurin, for her insight and willingness to find the deepest truth she knows and let everything else fall in place around it. As you know from the introduction, this book would not have existed without her. Thank you, too, to our daughters, Katie and Kara, for their ever-present love and enthusiastic exploration of their deepest truths. You are all so dear to me! Living the deepest truth I know with you is the love and joy of my life.

Notes, Comments and References

Introduction
Page ix. Excerpt from "The Journey" by Mary Oliver. Reprinted by permission from Grove Atlantic Press, as per representation by Salky Literary Management LLC. Copyright © 1986, 2017 by Mary Oliver with permission of Bill Reichblum.

Page x. My wife's book about her patients' extraordinary experiences is *Near Death in the ICU: Stories from patients near death and why we should listen to them*. Sloan Press, 2016.

Chapter 1: Who Am I, Anyway?
Page 9. The detailed description of "the deepest truth you know" is largely from my personal experience. Various religious traditions and other people who engage with inner wisdom may emphasize some aspects of the process more than others, or describe it differently.

Page 13. *Eat Pray Love*, by Elizabeth Gilbert. Bloomsbury Publishing PLC, 2007.

Page 13. *The Stargate Chronicles*, by Joseph McMoneagle. Hampton Roads Publishing, 2002.

Page 14. "Vontae Davis retired at halftime of an NFL game. That's just the beginning of his story." Adam Kilgore, The Washington Post, November 26, 2019.

Page 14. *A Hidden Wholeness: The Journey Toward an Undivided Life*, by Parker J. Palmer. John Wiley & Sons, 2009. All quotes from Parker Palmer are used with permission from the author.

Chapter 2: Trust

Page 21. Dr. Jerry Epps is also the author of several independently published books and programs, which are available on Amazon.com. They include *The Democracy Book*, *The Free Enterprise Book*, and *My Walks with God: Personal Stories of Unearned Grace*.

Page 29. In the time since I lived in the apartment next to it, the Quonset hut that housed the Oak Park auto parts and repair shop has been torn down and replaced with a pharmacy.

Chapter 3: Courage

Page 41. Richard Moss, MD, is the author of numerous books, including *The I That Is We: Awakening to Higher Energies Through Unconditional Love* (Celestial Arts, 1981) and *The Mandala of Being: Discovering the Power of Awareness* (New World Library, 2007).

Page 44. Lori Yadin is a Circle of Trust facilitator and honors wholistic living as a path to achieving human potential.

www.creatingsafespace.org

Chapter 4: Asking for Your Truth

Page 49. Information that might identify my psychotherapy clients has been changed to preserve their privacy.

Chapter 5: Understanding Inner Wisdom

Page 70. I first encountered the Old English root of the word "healing," *haelen*, and its implication of wholeness, in a talk given by Janet Quinn, Ph.D., RN, FAAN, an extraordinary healer and wonderfully insightful doctor of nursing. www.janetquinn.com

Page 74. *Listening Spirituality, Vol. 1: Personal Spiritual Practices Among Friends*, by Patricia Loring. Openings Press, 1997.

Page 75. *New Seeds of Contemplation*, by Thomas Merton. New Directions, 1961.

Page 75. *Immortal Diamond: The Search for Our True Self*, by Richard Rohr. Jossey-Bass, 2013.

Page 76. The "actualizing tendency" is defined in "A theory of therapy, personality and interpersonal relationships as developed in the client-centered framework," by Carl Rogers, in S. Koch (Ed.), *Psychology: A Study of Science* (Vol. 3, pp. 184–256). McGraw-Hill, 1959. It is also discussed in *A Way of Being*, first published by Houghton Mifflin, 1980.

Page 77. *A Hidden Wholeness: The Journey Toward an Undivided Life*, by Parker Palmer. Jossey-Bass, 2004.

Chapter 6: Mission and Purpose

Page 87. *Medicine as a Human Experience*, by David E. Reiser & David H. Rosen. University Park Press, 1984.

Page 98. *The Fearless Benjamin Lay: The Quaker Dwarf Who Became the First Revolutionary Abolitionist*, by Marcus Rediker. Beacon Press, 2017.

Chapter 7: Welcome, Truth

Page 111. The Circle of Trust® approach is described and discussed extensively in Parker Palmer's book, *A Hidden Wholeness: The Journey Toward an Undivided Life*, ibid. The Touchstones used to create safety in a Circle of Trust retreat, as well as the principles and practices that are followed to allow inner wisdom to come forward, can be explored at the website of the Center for Courage & Renewal. www.couragerenewal.org

Page 114. "The Way It Is" from *Ask Me: Selected Poems* is one of William Stafford's most beloved poems and was written less than a month before he died. Copyright © 1998 by William Stafford and the Estate of William Stafford. Reprinted with the permission of The Permissions Company, LLC, on behalf of Kim Stafford and Graywolf Press, graywolfpress.org.

Page 116. Parker Palmer's comment that a Circle of Trust can be created with even two or three people is from his book, *A Hidden Wholeness: The Journey Toward an Undivided Life*, ibid. Also note the similarity with Matthew 18:20: "For where two or three gather in my name, there I am with them."

Page 123. Larry Littlebird is a retreat leader, wisdom teacher, and the author of Hunting Sacred, Everything Listens: A Pueblo Indian Man's Oral Tradition Legacy. Western Edge Press, 2001.

Chapter 8: Opening to Life

Page 128. Meditation has been an important part of my own path, and I've written about a simple mindful practice that can help people cope with difficult life situations. *Simply Mindful: Reclaiming Your Life*. Sloan Press, 2018.

Chapter 9: Fully Alive

Page 148. Lighting a fire is a delicate balancing act in any case, but lighting a fire in the snow asks for additional care since the fire itself will create the very circumstances (meltwater) that will put it out.

Page 150. The excerpt from Mary Oliver's poem, "When Death Comes," is from her book, *New and Selected Poems*, Beacon Press, 1992. Reprinted by the permission of the Charlotte Sheedy

Literary Agency as agent for the author. Copyright © 1992, 2006, 2017 by Mary Oliver with permission of Bill Reichblum.

Appendix: Your Own Journey
Page 153. The five steps described here are based on my own life experience rather than a specific tradition. You might want to consider exploring silent Quaker worship, Circle of Trust retreats, Clearness Committees, prayer, or other practices that call to you.

About the Author

Albert Bellg helps people find clarity and courage in their work and personal lives. He is a husband and father, poet, psychologist, and retreat facilitator. He has written books on soccer tactics, storytelling in the medical world, and mindful practice.

www.ingramcontent.com/pod-product-compliance
Lightning Source LLC
Chambersburg PA
CBHW030437010526
44118CB00011B/674